Healing the Wounded Soul

By Rod Stevenson

Copyright © 2025 by Rod Stevenson

Published in the USA in 2025 by Present Truth Books. A division of Rivers of Living Water Ministries International 1550 E. Laketon Ave. Muskegon Michigan 49442

Printed in the United States of America All rights reserved. No part of this publication may be reproduced, stored in a retrieval system, or transmitted in any form or by any means-for example, electronic, photocopy, and recording-without the prior written permission of the publisher. The only exception is brief quotations in printed reviews.

ISBN: 978-0-9898493-3-3

Scripture is taken from the KING JAMES BIBLE ® Copyright © and the AMPLIFIED BIBLE ® Copyright ©

For current information about this book or booking information for Apostle Rod Stevenson please contact: ROLWMI Muskegon 1550 E Laketon Ave Michigan 49442 (231-206-4966)
Email rolwmuskegon@gmail.com
Website: http://www.rolwmuskegon.com

Table of Contents

Chapter 1 — 4
Steps to Healing the Wounded Soul

Chapter 2 — 29
Soul Wounds Are Like Tombs or Monuments

Chapter 3 — 41
The Glory, The Blood and The Light

Chapter 4 — 55
The Glory, The Blood And The Light to Heal Soul Woun

Chapter 5 — 71
Breaking the Strong Man and the Curse

Chapter 6 — 83
Hurt People Hurt People

Chapter 7 — 95
Identifying Strong Men and Their Functions

Chapter 8 — 105
The Strong Man of Rebellion, Rejection, and Witchcraft

Chapter 9 — 112
Dealing with The Assyrian Spirits

Chapter 10 — 123
The Blood and Light of Jesus

Chapter 11 — 137
Barriers to Hearing God Clearly

Chapter 12 — 150
Pillars of Inner Healing

Chapter 13 — 157
Pillars of Inner Healing Cont.

Chapter 1

Steps to Healing the Wounded Soul

As we begin this journey into healing the wounded soul, it's important to lay a foundation. Every human being is made up of three parts: spirit, soul, and body. When a person receives Jesus Christ as Lord and Savior, the spirit is regenerated — made completely new.

Paul says in **2 Corinthians 5:17**
Therefore if any man be in Christ, he is a new creature: old things are passed away; behold, all things are become new.

Yet many believers struggle with a pressing question: *If my spirit is new, why do I still battle sin?* Why do some Christians continue in fornication, adultery, lying, cheating, cursing, or living in habits that dishonor God — even though they love Him sincerely? Paul described this struggle in **Romans 7:18-20 (KJV):**
"For I know that in me (that is, in my flesh,) dwelleth no good thing: for to will is present with me; but how to perform that which is good I find not. For the good that I would I do not: but the evil which I would not, that I do. Now if I do that I would not, it is no more I that do it, but sin that dwelleth in me."

Every one of us can relate. There are things we want to do for God — we desire to pray, to live holy, to worship with passion — but often we cannot follow through. At the same time, there are things we hate — sins we wish we could overcome — yet we find ourselves repeating them. Why does this happen? The answer is this: our spirit is perfect, but our soul is not.

The soul is made up of three parts:
- The mind (how we think and reason).
- The will (our capacity to choose and decide).
- The emotions (our feelings, reactions, and desires).

While our spirit is instantly regenerated by Christ at salvation, our soul still carries scars, wounds, and damage from past experiences. These wounds often stretch back into childhood — traumas, abuses, words spoken over us, rejection from parents, molestation, violence, abandonment, and failures that left us broken.

Each wound becomes an open door, a place where the enemy gains access. These are entry points that demons use to influence, torment, and oppress believers. And unless these wounds are healed, we will continue to struggle — not because we are not saved, but because our soul remains wounded and vulnerable.

Why Christians Still Struggle

If you are a believer who has accepted Jesus Christ as Lord, your spirit has been regenerated. You are a new creation. But your soul — your mind, will, and emotions — still carries wounds from the past. These wounds explain why so many Christians struggle to walk in consistent victory.

Think about it. If salvation automatically solved everything, then why do believers still fall into adultery, fornication, lying, cheating, addictions, and anger? Why do Christians curse, gossip, and live in ways that grieve the Holy Spirit?

It is because the soul remains unhealed. The enemy has used life experiences — rejection, betrayal, abuse, and trauma — as entry points into the soul. These unhealed places give him access, and that access becomes a stronghold.

And remember this: we live in a demon-infested world. When Satan rebelled against God, a third of the angels fell with him. Those fallen angels became demons — and they now roam the earth in the billions. Their target is not your spirit (which belongs to God), but your soul.

Can Christians Have Demons?

Some people struggle with this concept. "If I'm saved, how can a demon touch me?"
The truth is this: Christians can have demons, not in their spirit, but in their soul or body.

Think about it. If demons couldn't affect Christians, then why do believers get sick? Every disease is rooted in sin and darkness. If sickness can touch the body of a Christian, then oppression can touch the soul of a Christian.

The key is this: the enemy has no authority over us unless we give him a place of agreement — unless there is something in us that he can attach to.

Jesus Himself confirmed this in **John 14:30 KJV:**
"Hereafter I will not talk much with you: for the prince of this world cometh, and hath nothing in me."

Satan searched for something in Jesus' soul — a wound, an open door, a point of agreement. But there was none. That's why the enemy could not control Him.

How Sin Wounds the Soul

Every sin we commit — and every sin committed against us — affects the soul. For example, sexual sins don't just affect the body. They also wound the soul.

Proverbs 6:32 KJV says:
"But whoso committeth adultery with a woman lacketh understanding: He that doeth it destroyeth his own soul."

When a person sins sexually, they defile their own soul. And when others sin against us — through rejection, abuse, or betrayal — those wounds lodge deep in our inner being.

Isaiah 1:6 (KJV) paints a vivid picture of what this looks like:
"From the sole of the foot even unto the head there is no soundness in it; but wounds, and bruises, and putrifying sores: they have not been closed, neither bound up, neither mollified with ointment."

This is what the soul looks like apart from the healing of Christ. Wounds, bruises, and open sores — never stitched up, never treated. And those wounds become doors for demonic influence.

A Personal Example in Ministry

I remember ministering to someone years ago. As I prayed, the Holy Spirit revealed that there were demons stationed like guards between this person's soul and their spirit. These demons blocked the passageway where the light of Jesus Christ wanted to shine.

The Lord instructed me to command those spirits to move. And when they were removed, the person was suddenly able to receive the Holy Spirit in a way they never had before.

Why? Because until that moment, demons were blocking access. Once forgiveness and repentance were released, the blockage was gone, and the Spirit of God entered freely.
This is why many believers find it so difficult to walk in victory. It is not that they don't love God. It is that their souls are wounded, and demons exploit those wounds.

The Cycle of Struggle

Maybe you can relate. Perhaps you've battled addictions — drugs, pornography, masturbation, adultery, or fornication. Maybe you've struggled with lying, gossip, or anger. You've tried to stop, you've repented, and you've promised God "never again" — only to fall back into the same patterns. That cycle doesn't mean you don't love God. It means your soul has been wounded and the enemy has gained a foothold.

Remember: Satan cannot touch your spirit. That belongs to God. But he can influence your soul — your thoughts, your desires, your emotions, and your will. That's why the soul must be healed.

How Wounded Souls Affect the Mind, Will, and Emotions

Your soul is made up of three parts: the mind, the will, and the emotions. When the soul is wounded, every one of these areas is impacted — and the results show up in daily life.

1. The Mind
When wounds lodge in the soul, they cloud the mind. This is why some people experience confusion, memory loss, or even mental breakdowns.

Today we see an alarming rise in dementia and Alzheimer's. Years ago, these conditions were rare. But now they're becoming increasingly common. Why? Because sin and wickedness are increasing in the earth, and the enemy is attacking the souls of men.

When a person's soul is wounded, the enemy exploits that vulnerability to torment the mind. That torment can manifest as forgetfulness, irrational fears, or mental instability.

2. The Will
Perhaps even more damaging is what wounds do to the will. A wounded soul robs believers of the very desire to seek God. Have you ever wondered why it seems so hard to get people to pray, read their Bibles, or worship consistently?

As a pastor, this used to frustrate me deeply. I would ask, *"Lord, why is it so difficult to get people to read Your Word? Why don't they have a will to serve You?"* And the Lord answered: *"Their souls are wounded."*

When the soul is wounded, people lose the will to love, the will to forgive, the will to worship, and even the will to come to church. They may want to desire God — but their wounded soul keeps them unstable and inconsistent.

3. The Emotions

Finally, the emotions. Wounds in the soul make it difficult to maintain stability. People become easily offended, easily angered, or easily discouraged. One moment they are on fire for God, ready to worship and serve. The next moment they are depressed, anxious, or ready to give up. These emotional highs and lows are not random — they are symptoms of an unhealed soul.

My Own Pastoral Struggle

Let me be transparent. There was a season in my ministry where I grew extremely frustrated. I would preach, teach, and encourage people, but they still didn't seem to grow. I kept asking God, *"Why can't I get my church to consistently read Your Word, to spend time with You, to pray with passion?"*

And the Lord showed me: *"Their souls are wounded. Until they learn how to use My Word and apply the tools and strategies I've given, they won't be able to heal. And until their souls are healed, they won't truly know Me."*

That revelation changed everything. I realized that before people could build a real relationship with God, their wounds had to be addressed. And the only way to heal those wounds is by applying the blood of Jesus and the light of His glory.

Why This Battle Matters

This is not a side issue. The healing of the soul is foundational to Christian life.
Without healing, believers will continue to:
Struggle with addictions and sins they hate.

- Live in cycles of emotional instability.
- Lack the will to pray, worship, or seek God.
- Remain vulnerable to demonic oppression.

But when the soul is healed, believers become strong, whole, and stable. They can walk in obedience, exercise authority over the enemy, and experience true intimacy with King Jesus.

Jesus the King and Dominion

The Bible calls Jesus King of kings and Lord of lords. Revelation 19 paints a powerful picture of Him: riding a white horse, clothed in a robe dipped in blood, crowned with many crowns, and followed by heavenly armies. Out of His mouth comes a sharp sword with which He judges and makes war. His rule is symbolized by a rod of iron—unbreakable, unstoppable authority.

When Scripture says He is *King of kings*, it doesn't just mean He is above earthly rulers. It means He is King over every demonic kingdom and principality. No spirit of lust, witchcraft, rebellion, or infirmity can stand against Him. He has triumphed over them all.
And here is the good news: when we carry His presence, His dominion extends through us. That means every kingdom of darkness is subject to the authority of Christ in us. But—and this is crucial—our ability to walk in that dominion is tied to the condition of our soul.

If your soul is wounded, you may know the truth in your spirit, but you will lack authority in practice. That's why so many believers remain stuck in cycles of defeat.

Testimony: My Uncle's Battle for His Soul

I saw this truth firsthand in my own family. I had an uncle who lived a life of partying—drinking, chasing women, living recklessly. He ignored the warnings of God for years. Eventually, his mind began to slip.

By the end of his life, it was as if the enemy had taken his soul captive. He sat around, chain-smoking, staring into space, barely functioning. Every once in a while, he'd snap back for a moment, speak clearly, and then drift off again.

The doctors couldn't explain it fully, but I knew spiritually what had happened: the enemy had gained ground through years of open doors. Sin had given demons legal access to wound and ultimately dominate his soul. This is why Scripture warns us so strongly. Sin is never harmless. Every compromise creates wounds, and wounds create entry points. And if they remain unhealed, the enemy will keep pressing until he gains control.

Why the Soul Matters

Our soul is made up of mind, will, and emotions. When it is healthy, we walk in freedom. But when it is wounded:
- Our mind becomes foggy, unstable, or even lost (as in dementia, breakdowns, or torment).

- Our will becomes weak, making obedience and discipline feel impossible.
- Our emotions swing wildly, leaving us controlled by fear, anger, or depression.

I remember asking the Lord once, "Why is it so hard to get people in church to simply read Your Word, pray, and love one another?" His answer was simple but profound: *"Because their souls are wounded."*

When your soul is broken, you may want to pray, but you can't stay focused. You may want to study the Word, but distraction takes over. You may want to forgive, but emotions flare up. Wounded souls create instability.

This is why soul healing is essential before we can walk in the fullness of relationship with God.

Wounded Souls & Authority

One of the Lord's greatest revelations to me was this: the condition of your soul directly affects your level of dominion. Think about it. If your soul is whole, demons have nothing in you. But if your soul is wounded, it creates "common ground" where the enemy can attack.

That's why Jesus said in **John 14:30 (KJV), "Hereafter I will not talk much with you: for the prince of this world cometh, and hath nothing in me."**

That's the goal: to reach a place where Satan comes looking, but finds nothing in us to grab onto. But most believers are far from that place, because they carry unhealed wounds—often from childhood or early life. Those wounds become tombs of remembrance that the enemy uses to trigger us again and again.

Testimony: My Brother Willie Digging the Well

I saw this reality in my own family while we were building my house years ago. My brother and I were digging a well together. It's hard work—you throw the digger down, pull it up, dump the sand, and repeat. After a while, he was taking his turn, and suddenly something strange happened. He stopped, burst into tears, and cried, *"No, I can't do this anymore!"* Then he ran into the garage weeping.

I was stunned. This was a grown man, nearly 60 years old at the time, breaking down like a child. As he composed himself, he shared what had happened: the act of digging had triggered a memory. He remembered when our grandfather ("Big Daddy") forced him as a child to dig a well under harsh conditions. That experience had left a wound buried deep inside his soul.

Decades later, in an ordinary moment, the environment and action of digging reopened that wound. It was as if he was transported back to being that hurting boy again. This is exactly how wounds in the soul operate. They are like monuments or tombs within us. When life touches the same environment, the wound "speaks," and we react—not out of present reality, but out of old pain. That's why people often overreact, shut down, or lash out in situations that don't seem to warrant it. The wound is speaking.

Romans 7: The Inner War

The Apostle Paul describes this reality in **Romans 7:20 (KJV):**

"Now if I do that I would not, it is no more I that do it, but sin that dwelleth in me."

Notice that phrase: *"fixed and operating in my soul."* Paul recognized that when he fell into sin he didn't want to commit, it wasn't his spirit agreeing—it was sin lodged in his soul, functioning like a living force.

That's why you can love Jesus with all your heart, yet still feel powerless over addiction, lust, anger, or fear. It's not that your spirit isn't born again. It's that your soul is wounded, and demons use those wounds as footholds to keep operating.

Strongholds and Kings

Jesus said in Matthew 12:29 that before you can plunder a strong man's house, you must first bind the strong man. That's why some Christians pray, fast, and cry out, but still see no breakthrough. They're trying to fight the "army" without ever dealing with the king that commands it.

I've seen it in deliverance ministry: sometimes you confront a demon and it won't budge. Why? Because the person has never dealt with the "king" over that area—the strong man ruling that particular kingdom. For example, there's a king over lust, a king over deception, a king over witchcraft. If you don't dethrone the king, the army stays.

That's why soul wounds matter so much. They give the strong man legal ground to stay.

Steps to Soul Healing

Healing your soul is not automatic. Salvation gives you eternal life in your spirit, but soul wounds must be intentionally brought into the presence of Christ. God has already provided everything through the cross — your role is to apply it.

Below are the steps that the Lord has given us in His Word to experience deep, lasting healing:

1. Identify the Wounds
You cannot heal what you will not face. Many believers keep their wounds hidden behind busyness, ministry, or denial. But hidden wounds fester; exposed wounds can be healed.

Pray like David did in **Psalm 139:23–24 (KJV):**
"Search me, O God, and know my heart: Try me, and know my thoughts: And see if there be any wicked way in me, And lead me in the way everlasting."

Ask the Holy Spirit to shine His light on the hidden places of your soul. Sometimes He will do this through Scripture, other times through dreams, through the words of a trusted friend, or even through the painful conflicts of life. Don't resist this process — welcome it.

Personal Example: I once prayed this very prayer during a season of ministry when I thought I was doing fine. The Lord revealed a deep wound of rejection from years earlier that was still shaping how I related to people. I didn't realize that the way I withdrew from others was not shyness but self-protection. When God uncovered it, I finally understood why I kept hitting the same relational walls — and that became the starting point of my healing.

2. Repentance & Forgiveness
Two of the most powerful keys to soul healing are repentance and forgiveness.
- Repentance means owning your sin — the rebellion, immorality, bitterness, or pride that has opened doors in your soul. Repentance is not just "feeling sorry," but turning away and inviting Christ to cleanse the wound.
- Forgiveness means releasing others who sinned against you. This is often the hardest step, because wounds usually come from people we trusted. But forgiveness is not excusing their actions; it is placing them in God's hands.

Without forgiveness, your wound remains open. With forgiveness, the enemy loses his legal right to torment you.

3. Apply the Blood of Jesus
After repentance and forgiveness, the next step is applying the blood of Jesus over your soul.

Romans 8:1 (KJV) promise:
"There is therefore now no condemnation to them which are in Christ Jesus, who walk not after the flesh, but after the Spirit."

The blood of Christ doesn't just forgive sin — it cleanses, remits, and removes condemnation. It silences the voice of the accuser and closes the legal case the enemy tries to hold against you.

Testimony: I remember ministering to someone who had been stuck in cycles of shame for years. They had repented many times, but they still felt unworthy. When they finally applied the blood — declaring out loud, "By the blood of Jesus I am forgiven, I am clean, and I am free" — the heaviness lifted. It was as if a courtroom verdict had been reversed, and their soul walked out free.

4. Access the Glory of God
Healing doesn't happen in theory; it happens in God's presence. His glory is His dwelling presence, the weight of who He is. We access this through worship, prayer, and surrender. When you lift your heart in worship, you are creating an atmosphere where the glory of God can rest upon your life. And in that glory, wounds are mended. Think of it this way: the presence of God is not just a comfort — it is a healing balm. When His glory rests, His light begins to touch the most broken parts of your soul.

5. Receive Healing Light
The final step is receiving the healing light of Christ.

Malachi 4:2 (KJV)declares:
"But unto you that fear my name shall the Sun of righteousness arise with healing in his wings; and ye shall go forth, and grow up as calves of the stall."

Jesus is the Sun of Righteousness. His light penetrates darkness, dissolves lies, and stitches wounds shut. He is Jehovah Rapha — the Lord who heals.

Imagine His light as beams shining into every corner of your soul: the childhood memory that still hurts, the fear that lingers, the anger that erupts, or the shame that whispers. As you invite His light in, healing begins.

Practical Exercise: In your prayer time, close your eyes and imagine standing before Jesus. See His face

shining like the sun (Revelation 1:16). Now picture His rays of light streaming into your heart, touching each wound. Speak out loud:
- *"Lord, shine Your light into my rejection."*
- *"Lord, heal the wound of fear."*
- *"Lord, close every door I opened through sin."*

Stay there until you sense peace replacing pain. That is His healing presence at work.
Healing is not always instant. For some wounds, it is a process. But every time you follow these steps, you are closing doors to the enemy and allowing the Lord to make your soul whole.

Sun = Brilliance of Light

The Scripture calls Him the Sun of Righteousness. Just as the physical sun floods the earth with light and life, Jesus shines with spiritual brilliance that drives out darkness. Light does not argue with darkness; it simply shines, and darkness disappears. When you allow Christ's light to shine into your soul, confusion, deception, and despair cannot remain.

Wings = The Glory Covering

The word *"wings"* in this verse comes from the Hebrew word *kanaph*, which means "the edge" or "corner" of a garment — specifically the prayer shawl (tallit) that Jewish men wore. The corners of that garment represented God's authority, protection, and covering. The prophecy points us to a powerful truth: healing is found in the covering glory of Christ. Under His wings, there is safety, deliverance, and restoration.

Healing = Remedy, Cure, Restoration

The word for *healing* in Hebrew is marpe — meaning medicine, remedy, cure, or stitching together. It is not just relief of symptoms; it is the mending of what is torn. When Christ shines His healing light, He is not just soothing your pain — He is closing the wound, curing the disease, and restoring wholeness.

Example: The Woman with the Issue of Blood (Mark 5:25–34)

A woman had been bleeding for twelve years. She had spent all her money on doctors and found no relief. She was ceremonially unclean, socially isolated, and physically broken. Yet she heard about Jesus.

Mark 5:27–29 (KJV) records:
"when she had heard of Jesus, came in the press behind, and touched his garment. For she said, If I may touch but his clothes, I shall be whole. And straightway the fountain of her blood was dried up; and she felt in her body that she was healed of that plague."

What did she touch? The kanaph — the corner of His garment. In other words, she touched the very place Malachi had prophesied healing would flow: the wings of His righteousness.

Notice something important: Jesus was not actively ministering to her. He didn't lay hands on her, give her a word, or stop to pray. Healing flowed out of Him because she accessed the principle of glory-light. She believed, she touched, and virtue flowed.

Application for Us

Faith unlocks the flow of healing light. The woman kept saying to herself, "If I just touch Him, I will be healed." Healing begins when you believe His light is enough. Healing flows from His presence, not formulas. She didn't follow a 10-step plan — she reached out in desperation, and His glory met her.

You can access His healing light today. You don't need Jesus physically in front of you to touch His garment. You can, in faith, reach out in prayer and touch His Word, His Spirit, and His presence. The same light shines now.

Personal Example: I once prayed with a man bound by chronic back pain for years. Medicine only dulled the ache. During worship, I encouraged him to picture himself reaching for the hem of Jesus' garment. As he did, tears streamed down his face. He whispered, "I feel warmth in my back." That warmth was the light of Christ's presence. By the end of that meeting, he was bending and moving with no pain for the first time in decades.

The principle is simple but profound: Healing comes not only when Christ actively ministers to you, but when you believe and reach for the light of His glory that always surrounds Him.

Living Under an Open Heaven

The miracles of Jesus consistently revealed one principle: when the heavens are open, the supernatural flows freely. His ministry was not random — it was patterned by moments when heaven's glory was manifested.

Jesus Looked to Heaven

- **Mark 7:34 (KJV)**— The Healing of the Deaf Man
  "And looking up to heaven, he sighed, and saith unto him, Ephphatha, that is, Be opened."

When Jesus healed the deaf man, the key action was *looking up to heaven*. His authority was connected to heaven's open flow.

- **Mark 6:41** — The Feeding of the 5,000
  "And when He had taken the five loaves and the two fish, He looked up to heaven, blessed and broke the loaves, and gave them to His disciples to set before them..."

A few loaves became a banquet because Jesus acknowledged the Source. Looking to heaven opened the way for multiplication.

The Principle

Miracles manifest when the heavens are open through worship and thanksgiving. Jesus modeled this: before He commanded, before He multiplied, He always acknowledged the Father. Thanksgiving and worship create alignment between earth and heaven.

The Bronze Serpent & Healing Light

The Word of God gives us a powerful picture of healing in Numbers 21:4–9. The Israelites had grown weary on their wilderness journey. They murmured, complained, and spoke against God and Moses. This sin of rebellion opened the door for judgment, and "fiery serpents" came among the people, biting them and causing many to die. Yet even in judgment, God provided a picture of mercy. He instructed Moses:

> **"Make thee a fiery serpent, and set it upon a pole: and it shall come to pass, that everyone that is bitten, when he looketh upon it, shall live." (Numbers 21:8, KJV)**

Moses obeyed and lifted up a bronze serpent on a pole. Whoever looked—really looked, not with a passing glance but with a steadfast gaze of faith—was healed instantly.

Symbolism of the Bronze Serpent

- The Pole = The authority of Christ. It represents the cross where Jesus bore sin and judgment.

- The Serpent = Sin judged. Jesus, though sinless, was "made to be sin for us" (2 Cor. 5:21). He bore the curse, so we could be redeemed from it.

- The Bronze = Judgment. In Scripture, bronze often symbolizes judgment (see the brazen altar in the tabernacle). The bronze serpent was sin already judged by God.

- The Looking = Faith. The Israelites were healed not by medicine or ritual but by looking intently upon God's provision.

This points us directly to **John 3:14–15**, where Jesus Himself applies this passage:

"And as Moses lifted up the serpent in the wilderness, even so must the Son of man be lifted up: That whosoever believeth in Him should not perish, but have eternal life."

The healing power was not in the bronze serpent itself, but in the principle of beholding. When we fix our gaze on Christ crucified—seeing Him as the One who took our sin, curse, wounds, and infirmities—the light of His glory penetrates our souls and heals us at the root.

Personal Reflection

I remember a time in my own life when the Lord showed me this truth. I was carrying a wound that kept resurfacing—anger from betrayal I thought I had already "moved past." But every time I saw that person, it stirred back up. One day, in prayer, the Lord brought me to this passage. He said, *"Stop staring at what they did to you. Fix your eyes on what I did for you."*

It was like a flood of light came over me. I realized I had been staring at the "bite" instead of the cross. And just like Israel in the wilderness, when I shifted my gaze, healing began to flow—not just to my emotions, but to the root of my soul.

Application for the Reader

Beloved, maybe you too have been bitten—by betrayal, rejection, abuse, or sin. The poison of those bites may still flow in your soul, producing pain and dysfunction. But hear the Word of the Lord:

- Stop staring at the wound. Fix your gaze on Christ crucified.
- See Him on the pole, bearing your curse.
- See His light and glory flowing from the cross into your wound.

This is the glory-light principle: healing comes when you behold Jesus, not yourself.

Practical Application for Today

The story of the bronze serpent is not just a historical event. It is a living principle for us today. Healing flows when we stop murmuring, stop staring at the poison, and start gazing at Christ. Let's bring this into practical, daily application.

1. Stop Murmuring and Complaining

The fiery serpents came upon Israel because of murmuring. Complaining opens the door to demonic "bites." Every time we grumble, criticize, or rehearse negativity, we agree with darkness instead of God's light.

Philippians 2:14–15 (KJV) says:
"Do all things without murmurings and disputings: that ye may be blameless and harmless, the sons of God, without rebuke, in the midst of a crooked and perverse nation, among whom ye shine as lights in the world"

Every complaint dims your light. Every word of gratitude strengthens it.
Practice: Each morning, write down three things you are thankful for before you start your day. Thankfulness closes the door to murmuring and opens the heavens over your soul.

2. Speak Words of Light, Life, and Healing
Proverbs 18:21 (KJV) says:
"Death and life are in the power of the tongue: and they that love it shall eat the fruit thereof."

If serpents represent poison, our words can either inject poison—or release healing medicine. When you declare God's Word, you release light into your atmosphere and soul.

Practice: Replace negative self-talk with Scripture. Instead of saying, "I'll never overcome this," say**, "Thanks be to God, who gives me the victory through our Lord Jesus Christ" (1 Cor. 15:57).**

3. Enter God's Presence Daily
The Israelites had to look at the serpent continually. Likewise, we must look at Jesus daily. Healing isn't a one-time glance; it is a lifestyle of beholding Him.
How do we do this?
- Worship: Lift your hands, sing, and acknowledge His presence.
- Scripture Meditation: Choose a "light Scripture" and repeat it until it fills your imagination.
- Quiet Waiting: Sit silently, visualizing His light beaming into your wounds.

Practice: Spend at least 15 minutes a day simply *beholding* Jesus—no requests, no agenda, just gazing in worship.

4. Build Family Altars of Prayer
Acts 2 shows us the early church "gathered in one accord." Miracles broke out because the glory rested on unity. Families and churches must create altars of prayer where the light of Christ can shine corporately. When families pray together, demonic serpents lose their grip. When churches worship together, heavens open over cities.

Practice: Set aside one night a week for family prayer and Scripture reading. Even if only for 20 minutes, make it a holy altar of light.

5. Meditate on "Light Scriptures"
Fill your soul with the Word of light until darkness has no room. Here are a few to begin with:
Malachi 4:2 – "The Sun of Righteousness shall arise with healing in His wings."

John 1:5 – "The light shineth in darkness; and the darkness comprehended it not."

Revelation 1:16 – "...*His face was like the sun shining in full strength.*"

Practice: Write one of these verses on a card. Carry it with you and read it aloud throughout the day.

Personal Testimony

I remember a season when my family began praying together at the dinner table—not just blessing the food, but reading Scripture and thanking God for specific things. At first, it felt awkward. But within weeks, I noticed a shift. Atmospheres of heaviness began to lift. Arguments lessened. Joy returned. Why?

Because we invited the glory-light into our home. Friend, what God did in my home, He can do in yours.

Summary for Application:

- Don't complain—be thankful.

- Speak healing words, not poisonous ones.

- Behold Jesus daily in worship and Scripture.

- Build family and corporate altars of prayer.

- Fill your soul with light Scriptures.

Chapter 2

Soul Wounds Are Like Tombs or Monuments

Before we can understand the healing of the demoniac, we need to notice what happened just before Jesus and His disciples arrived on that shore. In Mark 4:35–41 and Luke 8:22–25, Scripture records how Jesus said to His disciples, *"Let us go over to the other side of the lake."* It was a clear day. The waters were calm, good enough that even smaller boats launched out with them. No sailor in his right mind would push off in a storm, so we know the setting began in peace.

But suddenly, a furious storm arose. Mark describes it as a storm of hurricane force, while Luke adds a detail we might overlook: *"a whirlwind swept down on the lake."* This was no ordinary change in weather. It was an attack that came from above—spiritual forces stirring up the natural elements in order to block Jesus from reaching His assignment.

The disciples panicked, but Jesus rose and rebuked the storm. His authority calmed the winds and waves instantly. This reveals a powerful principle: demonic forces can hinder Kingdom assignments by disrupting the atmosphere. In this case, they attempted to use the weather itself as a weapon to prevent Jesus from arriving in the region where a powerful deliverance was about to take place.

Just as then, the enemy still tries to stir up storms in our lives—sometimes literally, other times through circumstances, distractions, confusion, or opposition—all designed to stop us from "crossing over" into the place of breakthrough and ministry that God has ordained.

Encounter with the Demoniac (Mark 5:1–20; Luke 8:26–39)

When Jesus and His disciples finally reached the other side of the lake, they were met by a man whose life was the very picture of torment. Both Mark 5 and Luke 8 tell us that he had been possessed by demons for a long time. He lived among the tombs, wore no clothes, and could not be restrained by chains. His existence was one of isolation, shame, and bondage.

As soon as he saw Jesus, the man cried out with a loud voice: "What have I to do with You, Jesus, Son of the Most High God?" (Mark 5:7). Luke's account adds another layer: "What have we in common?" (Luke 8:28, AMP).

That phrase is key. Demons always look for legal ground—something inside a person's soul that gives them a foothold. If there is "something in common" with their nature—an unhealed wound, an unresolved sin, an open doorway—they cling to it as their right to remain.

This is why deliverance and healing are often connected. In some cases, Jesus first cast out the spirits, and only then could healing flow. At other times, He healed directly. But the pattern shows us that demonic influence can cause or block physical healing.

Today, many believers pray endlessly for healing, yet they see no breakthrough. The sickness lingers, the bondage continues, and discouragement grows. What they don't always realize is that the real issue may not be physical at all—it may be spiritual. Some battles require deliverance before healing can manifest.

This is why Jesus' ministry was never just about physical healing or just about deliverance—they were often two sides of the same coin. He brought complete freedom: spirit, soul, and body.

Application: We must learn to discern. If you've prayed for healing again and again without breakthrough, it may be time to ask the Holy Spirit to reveal if there is a demonic foothold at work. Healing will not flow freely until the legal ground is broken and the stronghold is cast out. Deliverance clears the way for God's power to restore completely.

Soul Wounds as Tombs / Monuments

When Scripture describes the demoniac living among the tombs, there is more here than just a location. The word tomb in its root meaning refers to remembrance—a monument set up to recall an event continually. A tomb is not only a place of death; it is also a place of memory.

This is a picture of the soul. Wounds, traumas, and unresolved pain can become monuments within us—places where memories are revisited again and again, even decades later. These monuments stand as reminders of what was lost, what was done, or what we suffered, and they continue to influence how we feel, think, and even respond in the present.

I can remember one experience from my own college years. Something had happened back then that I thought I had left far behind. But years later, while in prayer, the Holy Spirit brought that memory back to the surface. To my surprise, I didn't just remember it—

I felt the same emotions rise up as though it had only happened yesterday. That was a sign to me: this was not just a memory, but a wound. It was still alive inside of me, and God was calling it out for healing.

Another example came through a testimony involving one of my brothers. We were digging a well on family property, and the act itself stirred something deep within him. Old memories resurfaced that had been buried for decades, and they triggered powerful emotions. Until that moment, none of us realized how deeply those past events had marked him. That experience showed me how family wounds can lie dormant for years—covered up and forgotten—until God allows something to bring them into the open.

Principle: When the Holy Spirit brings a memory back to your mind—especially if it stirs strong emotions—it is not to torment you. It is His way of showing you an area that still needs healing. It is never safe to simply dismiss it and say, "I'm fine, I forgave them, I don't think about it anymore." If the Spirit brings it up, it's because you are not fine. God in His mercy is pointing to the very place where His light and healing need to enter.

Isaiah 1:1-7 — The Nation's Wounds

The prophet Isaiah paints a sobering picture of God's people. God Himself says, "I have nourished and brought up sons, and they have rebelled against Me" (Isaiah 1:2). He raised them, He nurtured them, He cared for them—but they turned away.

What strikes me here is that He calls them His children, yet He says they do not know Him. They lacked relationship. They did not recognize His voice, His ways, or His heart.

This is not just Israel's problem in Isaiah's day—it is the condition of much of the Church today. Many claim the name of Christ, but they do not know Him. They know religion. They know church culture. But they do not know His ways. They have not cultivated intimacy.

Think about the relationship between a father and son. My son knows me. He knows what I like, what I don't like, what I allow, and what I forbid. That knowledge comes from closeness, from intimacy. Without relationship, that knowledge doesn't exist. And this is exactly what Isaiah says of God's people—they were His children, but they didn't truly know Him.

Now, let me pause and make a generational application. In many communities—especially within the African-American community—we see a crisis of absent fathers. Sons and daughters grow up without the presence, affirmation, and guidance of a father. And because of that, when it comes time to approach God as Father, they struggle. They don't know how to be intimate with Him because they never had that model on earth. Instead of receiving correction as love, they interpret it as rejection. Instead of resting in His presence, they feel abandoned. That wound carries into their spiritual walk.

Isaiah goes on to describe the condition in verses 5–6: "The whole head is sick, the whole heart is faint. From the sole of the foot even to the head, there is no soundness in it—but wounds and bruises and putrefying sores. They have not been closed, bound up, or soothed with ointment."

Notice the language. The head is sick—that speaks to leadership. When leaders are spiritually unhealthy, the people suffer. And the heart is faint—that's the soul: the mind, the will, and the emotions. It is weary, feeble, unstable.

Then Isaiah says the wounds are untreated. No ointment. No balm. No healing process has been applied. These are open sores, exposed to infection, never bound up, never soothed.

This is exactly the picture of so many believers today—walking around with open, untreated soul wounds. They are saved in spirit but broken in soul, and because no remedy has been sought, the wounds remain.

Need for Healing Balm (Isaiah 1:6–7)

Isaiah gives us a picture that is as relevant today as it was in his day: "From the sole of the foot even to the head, there is no soundness in it, but wounds, and bruises, and putrefying sores: they have not been closed, neither bound up, neither mollified with ointment." (Isaiah 1:6).

The imagery is clear—these are untreated wounds. Bruises that have not been pressed out. Bleeding stripes that have never been bound. Sores that have never been soothed with oil or balm. In other words, God's people are walking around in pain, but no healing process has been applied.

Prophetically, this is a picture of the wounded soul of the Church. Yes, people are saved in spirit. Yes, they know Jesus as Savior. But in the soul—mind, will, and emotions—they are still carrying injuries. Past trauma. Deep rejection. Abandonment. Betrayal. Abuse. Disappointment. Fear. These unhealed wounds remain wide open, and Isaiah says they stink—they are festering.

Now here's the question: Why aren't believers walking in intimacy, in healing, and in wholeness the way God desires? Why do we see so much bondage in the Church—cycles of sin, instability, broken relationships, and lack of power?

The answer is right here: unhealed wounds provide entry points for the enemy. When pain is not brought to the Cross, when rejection is not surrendered to the Father, when memories are not healed by the glory-light of Christ, they remain doors. And the enemy only needs a door to gain access.

This is why people can be faithful in church attendance, even serving in ministry, yet still live under oppression. They are saved, but not whole. Their wounds become monuments in the soul, and until those wounds are treated with the healing balm of Jesus—the Sun of Righteousness rising with healing in His wings (Malachi 4:2)—they will keep bleeding into every area of life.

God is not content to leave His children in that condition. He desires to pour in oil and wine, like the Good Samaritan (Luke 10:34). He desires to bind up the brokenhearted (Isaiah 61:1). He desires to apply His own balm, His glory, His light, until the wounds are closed and the soul can prosper.

2 Corinthians 4:1-6 — Exposing the Soul

Paul gives us a clear window into the battleground of the soul in 2 Corinthians 4:1-6. He speaks of the ministry of reconciliation, of holding fast to endurance, and of refusing to give in to weariness. But it is verse

2 in the Amplified Bible that brings this to light in a powerful way:

"We have renounced disgraceful ways—secret thoughts (mind), feelings (emotions), desires (will)—and underhandedness, the methods and arts that men hide through shame. We refuse to deal craftily or to adulterate or handle dishonestly the Word of God, but we state the truth openly, clearly, and candidly."

Do you see what Paul does here? He defines the soul for us: the mind (thoughts), the emotions (feelings), and the will (desires). That is the battleground. This is the place where the enemy looks for access. This is also the place where shame hides.

The battleground of the soul is hidden shame and unhealed wounds. These are the things we do not talk about, the things we would never admit to anyone, the things that are so covered over in secrecy we hope they never come up again. Yet Paul says those are exactly the things that must be renounced, exposed, and brought into the light of Christ.

Personal Testimony: The Sexual Vow Spirit

There was a time when the Holy Spirit exposed this in me in a way I'll never forget. I was watching a television show—one of those crime dramas. A rapist was pursuing a woman. Now, I was saved, born again, washed in the blood. But I found myself identifying with the rapist. I was actually urging him on: "Get up, get up, get her."
Suddenly the Holy Spirit stopped me. It was as if He pressed pause in the Spirit. He asked me: "Why are you identifying with the rapist? Why are you in agreement with that?"

And in that moment, I was shaken. Why was I? I had no desire for that in my conscious life. Yet there was something in me—a hidden wound from my dysfunctional upbringing, things I had been exposed to at a young age that I should never have seen—that had given the enemy common ground. A spirit had found a resting place in an unhealed part of my soul.

The revelation was clear: this was not who I was in Christ. This was a wound, and this was a spirit that had to go. I repented, renounced it, and brought it before the Cross. I crucified that spirit and rejected the vow it tried to hold over me. Deliverance came the moment it was exposed and confessed.

Application for Believers Today

Here's the principle: many believers unknowingly identify with evil through entertainment or hidden thoughts. They don't realize that when they find themselves cheering for the villain, lusting after an image, or imagining how they would "do it better" in a crime scene, it's not harmless. It reveals an unhealed wound or an area where the enemy has common ground.

Hidden shame, secret thoughts, and old sins must be renounced and confessed. We cannot cover them, excuse them, or bury them. They must be dragged into the light of Christ. Only then can the power of the Cross break them.

Deliverance begins where exposure happens. What the light exposes, the blood of Jesus cleanses.

The Power of Truth and Transparency (2 Corinthians 4:2)

Paul continues in 2 Corinthians 4:2 with these words: *"We state the truth openly, clearly, and candidly."*

There is a principle here that is life-changing: when sin is exposed, its sting is gone. As long as it stays in the dark, hidden and covered, it maintains its grip. But the moment it is brought into the light of truth, its power is broken.

That is why testimony becomes a weapon. Once you are delivered from something, you can speak about it openly. You are not ashamed, because the shame was nailed to the Cross with Christ. Your testimony now becomes a declaration of the Lord's victory, and that very testimony is what God uses to set others free.

But if we are still bound, if we still carry hidden chains, then we cannot testify freely. We avoid certain topics. We keep silent when God might be prompting us to speak. That silence is proof that the enemy still has a hold.

Confession is the door to freedom. When we confess — whether to God in prayer, or to a trusted brother or sister in Christ — the secrecy is removed. And with secrecy gone, the enemy loses his ground. Deliverance follows.

This is why James wrote:
"Confess your faults one to another, and pray for one another, that ye may be healed. The effectual fervent prayer of a righteous man availeth much." (James 5:16)

Confession breaks the secrecy, removes the shame, and allows healing to flow.

Blinding of the Mind (2 Corinthians 4:3–6)

Paul warns us in **2 Corinthians 4:3–4 (KJV):**

"But if our gospel be hid, it is hid to them that are lost: In whom the god of this world hath blinded the minds of them which believe not, lest the light of the glorious gospel of Christ, who is the image of God, should shine unto them."

Here we see that the battleground is the mind. The enemy knows if he can keep your mind blinded, you will remain in darkness. You can sit in church for years, hear truth every Sunday, and yet never see it transform your life. Why? Because darkness prevents truth from entering.

But Paul continues:

"For God, who said, 'Light shall shine out of darkness,' is the One who has shone in our hearts to give the Light of the knowledge of the glory of God in the face of Christ." (2 Cor. 4:6)

The light of the gospel reveals Christ's glory. Healing requires both the exposure to light and the experience of His glory. When the light shines, deception breaks. When His glory fills us, wounds are healed, strongholds are shattered, and intimacy with Christ is restored.

This is our inheritance. Paul tells us in Ephesians 2:6 that we are already "seated in heavenly places with Christ Jesus." That means every believer has legal access to the atmosphere of glory. And in the presence of His glory, deliverance and healing flow.

Application & Call to Action

- Ask the Holy Spirit to reveal hidden wounds and monuments. He will often bring back a memory or stir an old emotion — not to condemn you, but to show you where healing is needed.

- Do not ignore what resurfaces. If it comes up, it means God is targeting it for healing. What you bury will stay alive, but what you bring to the light will be healed.

- Bring wounds to Jesus and allow His glory-light to heal them. Invite Him into that memory, that emotion, that wound. See His light shining there, dissolving the darkness.

- Remember: Deliverance often comes first, then healing follows. True deliverance always leads to healing, wholeness, freedom, and intimacy with Christ.

- Daily practice:

— Sit in God's presence and welcome His light.
— Meditate on His Word until it fills your mind with truth.
— Renounce hidden shame and refuse secrecy — what is in the light cannot bind you.
— When you live this way, you will not only walk in freedom, but you will carry light and glory into the lives of others.

Chapter 3

The Glory, The Blood and The Light

Paul captures the struggle of the human soul when he writes:

"For I know that nothing good lives in me, that is, in my flesh [my human nature, my worldliness — my sinful capacity]. For the willingness [to do good] is present in me, but the doing of good is not. For the good that I want to do, I do not do, but I practice the very evil that I do not want. But if I am doing the very thing I do not want to do, I am no longer the one doing it [that is, it is not me who acts], but the sin nature which lives in me." (Romans 7:18-20 AMP)

This passage brings us to the very heart of the battle of the soul. Even a man as anointed and Spirit-filled as Paul acknowledged that there was a conflict raging within. He had the desire to do good, but something inside kept pulling him back into cycles of sin and defeat.

The reason is found in how God has designed us. The soul is made up of three parts: the mind, the will, and the emotions. When wounds form in these areas — from personal sin, from the sins of others, or from painful life experiences — they leave open doors. And wherever there is an open door, the enemy looks for access.

A wounded soul is like a wall with cracks in it. It might still be standing, but it is vulnerable to attack. Demonic influence looks for those cracks. This is why unresolved wounds become such dangerous entry points.

For example, wounds in the area of sexuality often lead to cycles of bondage. A person may desperately want to break free from lust, pornography, or sexual sin, but the hidden wound in the soul — perhaps rooted in abuse, rejection, or a past relationship — provides legal ground for the enemy to keep reintroducing temptation. The cycle repeats until the wound itself is healed.

Paul described this as a principle of sin fixed and operating within him. It was not merely that he occasionally stumbled; it was that something deep within his inner life kept producing the same fruit of failure. Many believers can relate: "Why do I keep falling into the same trap, even though I don't want to?"

The answer is that soul wounds must be healed if the cycle of repeated sin is to be broken. Without healing, we keep fighting symptoms while the root cause remains untouched. But when the Holy Spirit is invited to search out those wounded places, expose them to the light of Christ, and apply the blood of Jesus, the cracks are closed, and the enemy loses his foothold.

Prosperity of the Soul (3 John 1:2)

John prayed a blessing that every believer still needs to hear today:

"Beloved, I pray that you may prosper in every way and that your body may keep well, even as [I know]

your soul keeps well and prospers." (3 John 1:2 AMP)

This verse reveals a foundational truth: our health and prosperity in life are directly tied to the condition of our soul. The mind, the will, and the emotions — when healed and aligned under the Lordship of Christ — set the stage for wholeness in every other area of life.

Areas of Soul Prosperity

Mind — The healthy, prosperous mind is renewed daily by the Word of God. Without this renewal, the mind drifts back into old patterns of thinking, negativity, fear, or lust. Prosperity of the mind comes when our thoughts are shaped by Scripture and truth.

Will — The prosperous soul is one whose will has been surrendered and aligned with God's will. A carnal will craves entertainment, worldly approval, and temporary pleasures. For example, hours can be wasted binge-watching reality shows or feeding on content that does nothing for the spirit. By contrast, a sanctified will begins to hunger for the things of God: His Word, His presence in worship, His mission to reach nations, and His call to make disciples.

Emotions — When emotions prosper, they are no longer tossed around by every circumstance. Instead, they are mastered under the peace of Christ. Fear, anxiety, and anger are replaced with joy, confidence, and rest. This doesn't mean emotions are denied — it means they are healed and governed by the Spirit.

Testimony: Staying Sharp in the Word

One of the sweetest joys I have found is in discussing Scripture with my children. There is something powerful about hearing them ask questions, wrestle with truth, and apply the Word in their own lives. Every conversation not only blesses them, but also keeps me sharp and rooted in God's Word. It reminds me that prosperity of the soul isn't about what we gain externally, but what we are able to reproduce in others through our walk with God. When your soul is prospering, it naturally spills over into your home, your family, and your relationships.

Application

When the soul is healthy, the effects touch every part of life. Physical health often improves because stress, fear, and bitterness are removed. Financial prosperity flows more freely because decisions are made with clarity, discipline, and Kingdom purpose. Above all, intimacy with God deepens, and from that relationship comes joy, peace, and strength that no circumstance can take away. The principle is simple yet profound: when your soul prospers, your life prospers.

Long-Term Effects of Unhealed Souls

When soul wounds are left untreated, the effects don't simply fade with time — they intensify. Many of the long-term health crises we see today can often be traced back to early sin patterns or unresolved emotional wounds.

We are witnessing an alarming rise in conditions such as dementia, Alzheimer's, schizophrenia, and bipolar disorder. While not every case is spiritual in origin, many are deeply tied to brokenness in the soul and generational patterns of sin that were never brought under the healing power of Christ.

The Bible makes this clear in **Galatians 6:7:**
"Be not deceived; God is not mocked: for whatsoever a man soweth, that shall he also reap."

Sin patterns left unchecked sow destructive seeds in the body and mind. For example:

- Adultery and sexual sin open the door to cycles of shame, guilt, and self-loathing that break down both mental health and physical well-being.

- Rebellion against authority and rejection of parents can create deep root systems of bitterness and alienation, which later manifest in emotional disorders or strained relationships.

- Unforgiveness and resentment fester like toxins in the soul, eventually showing up as anxiety disorders, depression, or even physical illness.

What starts as "just a wound" in the emotions or mind can, over years, build into a fortress of torment. This is why we see people later in life consumed by paranoia, trapped in cycles of confusion, or overtaken by sickness of the body that seems unexplainable to doctors.

The Principle of Reaping

When we allow wounds to remain unhealed, we give Satan legal ground to build strongholds. Over time, those strongholds yield a harvest — not of life, but of destruction. The principle of sowing and reaping is not only about finances or blessings; it applies to the soul as well. Seeds of sin or bitterness, if not uprooted, eventually bear fruit in broken minds, diseased bodies, and fractured lives.

Healing Brings Renewal

But here is the good news: healing of the soul leads to restoration in every dimension. When the soul is healed, stress is released, the mind is renewed, and the body often begins to recover. Doctors will testify to the power of peace and joy in improving physical health. Scripture testifies even more clearly — when God heals the brokenhearted and binds up their wounds (Psalm 147:3), life and vitality flow again.

Many testimonies bear witness to this truth: as people forgive, repent, and release past pain to Jesus, not only do their hearts lighten, but their physical health improves. Blood pressure stabilizes, depression lifts, sleep is restored, and in some cases, even long-term diseases lose their grip.

Restored Prosperity

The soul is the engine of our life. When it is weighed down, the entire life suffers. But when it prospers, every other area prospers. Healing of the soul is not just about inner peace; it is about restoring wholeness of mind, stability of emotions, and strength of body. The Lord is calling His people not to accept decline, torment, or disease as "normal aging," but to believe Him for a healed soul that produces a fruitful and prosperous life — even into old age.

Steps to Soul Healing
- Identify Wounds

Invite the Holy Spirit to search the heart, as David prayed:
"Search me, O God, and know my heart; try me, and know my anxious thoughts." (Psalm 139:23).

Wounds are often hidden beneath years of denial or shame. The Spirit reveals what we would otherwise ignore.

- Repentance & Forgiveness

Healing requires both repentance for our own sins and forgiveness for the sins committed against us. Repentance breaks our agreement with sin; forgiveness removes bitterness that keeps wounds open.

- Apply the Blood of Jesus

The blood cleanses the soul, remits sin, and removes condemnation.
"There is therefore now no condemnation to those who are in Christ Jesus." (Romans 8:1).

The blood not only covers but restores, removing the enemy's legal right to torment.

- Access the Glory of God

Healing is found in His presence. Through worship, prayer, and surrender, the glory of God overshadows the wounded areas. The glory carries the atmosphere of heaven, releasing peace and renewal into broken souls.

- Receive the Light of Christ

Malachi 4:2 promises: "But for you who fear My name, the Sun of Righteousness will rise with healing in His beams."

His light penetrates wounds, burning away infection, stitching them shut, and sealing them with wholeness. Healing flows not by our striving but by exposure to His radiant light.

Principle: The soul is healed when wounds are exposed, repented of, covered by the blood, and bathed in His glory and light. This is the path from bondage to freedom, from torment to peace.

Healing Light in Scripture

(Malachi 4:2) "But for you who fear My name, the Sun of Righteousness shall arise with healing in His wings and beams."

- Sun (S-U-N)

Symbol of brilliance, radiance, and life-giving rays of light. Christ revealed as the true light who dispels darkness (John 1:5).

- Wings (Hebrew: kanaph)

Literally means edge, extremity, corner of a garment. In Jewish tradition, refers to the corners of the prayer shawl (tallit), representing covering, covenant, and authority.

Prophetically speaks of the glory covering of God.

- Healing (Hebrew: rapha)

Remedy, cure, restoration. Picture of wounds being stitched shut and fully mended. Not just physical healing but wholeness of soul and spirit.

- Symbolism of Light

Light drives out darkness; no shadow can remain where light shines. Healing comes as His glory light penetrates hidden wounds.

- Prophetic Picture

The cherubim over the Ark of the Covenant spread their wings, covering the mercy seat. From that place of glory, beams of divine light radiated. Malachi's prophecy points to Jesus as the Sun of Righteousness whose wings/beams release healing and deliverance.

Principle: Healing is not just a process—it is the result of encountering the radiant glory of Jesus. His light penetrates the darkest wounds, His covering protects, and His power restores.

Woman with the Issue of Blood (Mark 5:25-34)

- Her Condition

Suffered for 12 years with continual bleeding. Not only wounded in body, but also in finances — she had spent all she had on physicians. Still no cure, leaving her weak, rejected, and ceremonially unclean.

- Her Act of Faith

She pressed through the crowd despite her condition. Reached out and touched the kanaph — the hem, the edge of Jesus' garment (same word from Malachi 4:2, "wings"). This represented her contact with His covering, covenant, and glory.

- The Flow of Virtue/Light

Immediately, virtue (power, Dunamis) flowed out of Jesus. This wasn't just physical energy—it was glory-light penetrating her wound. Healing was instant, visible, undeniable.

- Jesus' Response

"Who touched me?" — He wasn't asking about physical contact, but who connected with His glory by faith. The disciples only saw the crowd pressing, but Jesus discerned the one who touched Him in spirit.

- Result

The woman was not only healed physically, but her dignity and identity were restored. Jesus called her "Daughter" — a public affirmation of acceptance after years of shame.

- Application

Healing and restoration come by contact with His light and glory through faith.

Just as she touched His garment, we touch His presence in worship, prayer, and the Word. His virtue still flows today into wounded bodies, finances, emotions, and souls.

Living Under an Open Heaven (Mark 7:32–35; Mark 6:41)

In Mark 7, we see Jesus healing the deaf man. He thrust His fingers into the man's ears, spat on his tongue, and then looked up to heaven, commanding, "Be opened!" This command was not only directed at the man's ears but at the heavens themselves. When the heavens are open, miracles begin to flow unhindered. The same principle is true today. During a crusade in Africa, a deaf woman came forward for prayer. Following Jesus' example, hands were placed in her ears and the same words were spoken: "Be opened!" Instantly she fell under the power of God, rose up, and her ears were opened. The miracle came not by human power, but because heaven itself had been opened over that moment.

The feeding of the 5,000 in Mark 6 shows the same principle. Faced with a multitude and very little provision, Jesus looked up to heaven, blessed, and gave thanks. Out of that worship and thanksgiving, the heavens opened, the glory of God was released, and supernatural provision multiplied until every person was fed and satisfied. The lesson is clear: worship and gratitude open the heavens, draw down the glory, and release miracles.

This is what Jesus meant by the "teaching of the loaves." The disciples saw the miracle but missed the principle. They thought it was about bread, but it was really about learning how to access the glory realm. Provision, healing, and deliverance do not flow until the heavens are opened. The atmosphere of glory must be created before miracles manifest. Worship, thanksgiving, and faith are the keys that bring heaven down to earth.

Application: Family Prayer & Open Heavens

After teaching on healing and deliverance, a witchcraft attack came against the family. Each member began to feel the effects—fear entered the children's rooms, physical affliction struck, and an atmosphere of oppression settled over the house. In that moment, the Holy Spirit brought Acts 2 to remembrance: "they were all together in one accord." Rather than praying separately, the family gathered as one, forming a family altar of prayer. As they lifted their voices together, the power of the attack was broken, peace returned to the home, and the presence of God filled the atmosphere.

This experience revealed an important principle: family and corporate altars open the heavens and release God's glory. When unity is established in prayer and worship, the enemy's assignments are destroyed. Just as open heavens bring miracles in public ministry, they also secure protection, healing, and peace within the home. Families who gather to pray together create an atmosphere where God's glory can dwell and where His kingdom reigns over every area of life.

The Bronze Serpent (Numbers 21:4–9)

When Israel murmured and complained against God and Moses, fiery serpents were released among them, and many were bitten and died. Their grumbling opened a doorway for demonic bites, revealing how dangerous complaining is to the soul. In response, God instructed Moses to lift up a bronze serpent on a pole. Whoever fixed their eyes intently upon it lived.

This was more than a physical cure—it carried prophetic symbolism. The pole represented the authority of Christ. The serpent represented sin judged and defeated. The bronze image, lifted high, became a focus point through which the glory of God was revealed. As the people gazed steadily upon it, the light of His presence brought healing.

Jesus later explained this mystery in **John 3:14–15: "As Moses lifted up the serpent in the wilderness, so must the Son of Man be lifted up, that whoever believes in Him may have eternal life."** The application for us is clear: when we fix our eyes on Christ crucified—on His finished work at the cross—the poison of sin and the wounds of our soul are healed. His glory and light flow into every place we focus upon Him, bringing deliverance, restoration, and life.

Practical Application

The path to soul healing begins with practical obedience. First, stop murmuring and complaining, as these open the door to serpents that bite. Instead, choose to speak words of life—words that release healing, prosperity, and hope. Make it a daily practice to enter God's presence through worship and Scripture meditation, allowing His glory to surround and transform you. Build family and corporate altars of prayer, just as the early church gathered together in one accord. In these altars, the heavens open, and God's glory is released. Anchor your meditation in "light Scriptures" such as Malachi 4:2, John 1:5, and Revelation 1:16. As you focus on these truths, the light of Christ will penetrate soul wounds, bringing restoration and wholeness where darkness once ruled.

Closing Exhortation

Remember this: Jesus carried our wounds so that we don't have to live bound by them. His glory and His light come to stitch shut the places in our soul where sin once left us broken and open. Healing flows when we meditate on Christ as the Light and allow the beams of His glory to shine into the deepest parts of our being. Therefore, I exhort you—this week, set aside intentional time to be with Jesus. Meditate on the light Scriptures. Worship Him. Sit in His presence. And as you do, expect His light to heal, to deliver, and to restore you into intimacy and freedom in Him.

Chapter 4

The Glory, The Blood and The Light to Heal Soul Wounds

The key scripture for this teaching is found in **Malachi 4:2: "But unto you who revere and worshipfully fear My name shall the Sun of Righteousness arise with healing in His wings and His beams." (AMP).**

This verse opens a prophetic picture that points directly to Christ. In the Old Testament the Word is concealed, but in the New Testament the Word is revealed. When the two are read together, they strengthen one another and bring a fuller revelation of God's intention. Scripture always interprets scripture, and the Old and the New work hand in hand like mirrors reflecting the same light.

As the verse was read aloud from the Amplified Bible, the imagery became clear—freedom, joy, and wholeness. The picture is one of release: calves leaping from the stall, healed and set free to run and rejoice. This is the joy that comes when the soul is healed.

Notice that the prophet says "Sun"—spelled S-U-N, not S-O-N. This imagery speaks of beams of light, brilliance, and radiance. Just as the natural sun releases powerful rays, the "Sun of Righteousness" shines beam of healing light into the deepest places of the human soul.

The word translated "wings" comes from the Hebrew kanaph (Strong's 4832), meaning the corner or edge of a garment—particularly the prayer shawl, or tallit. Symbolically, this represents the covering of God's glory. Thus, Malachi's prophecy reveals that healing flows from contact with the glory and light of Christ, just as rays from the sun bring warmth, life, and renewal.

The Woman with the Issue of Blood (Mark 5:25–34)

One of the clearest demonstrations of Malachi's prophecy is seen in the story of the woman with the issue of blood. Mark 5:25–34 tells us she had suffered for twelve long years, spending everything she had on physicians and treatments, yet her condition only grew worse. She was not only physically afflicted but emotionally and socially wounded—isolated, drained, and desperate.

But when she heard about Jesus, faith rose in her heart. She pressed through the crowd with one thought: *"If I can only touch the hem of His garment, I will be made whole."* What she actually touched was the *kanaph*—the corner of His prayer shawl. Spiritually, she was reaching for the covering of glory that Malachi 4:2 describes.

The moment she touched it, something remarkable happened. Power—virtue—flowed out of Jesus and into her body. Scripture says her bleeding stopped immediately, healed at the very source of her affliction. What makes this miracle so striking is that Jesus Himself was not consciously "trying" to heal her. He wasn't laying hands on her or releasing a prayer of faith. The healing came simply through contact with the glory and light that rested upon Him.

When Jesus turned and asked, *"Who touched Me?"* He wasn't asking about physical contact—many had brushed against Him in the crowd. He was asking about spiritual contact. One woman had reached past the natural into a spiritual principle. She accessed the glory and the light of the Lord Jesus Christ by faith, and it brought instant wholeness to her life.

This is the same principle available to us today. Healing doesn't always require a minister's touch, a dramatic moment at the altar, or even someone intentionally praying over us. Healing flows from contact with His glory-light—when by faith we press into His presence and "touch" the covering of His power.

Meaning of Healing (Rapha / Marpe)

When **Malachi 4:2 says the *Sun of Righteousness will rise with healing in His wings*,** the word used for *healing* is rich with meaning. In Hebrew, the word is marpe, which speaks of remedy, cure, restoration, and even soundness of mind. It is not just physical recovery—it is wholeness of the soul and spirit as well.

The root word is rapha, which literally means *to mend by stitching*. It paints the picture of a skilled physician carefully closing up an open wound so that it can heal properly. This is why one of God's covenant names is Jehovah Rapha—"The Lord Who Heals." He is the divine physician who not only cures our sickness but also stitches up the soul wounds that have left us spiritually bleeding.

Think about it this way: in the natural, if someone suffers a deep cut, a bandage isn't enough. The wound must be stitched shut so it can close and restore properly. In the same way, the wounds of rejection, betrayal, abuse, or sin in our lives cannot be ignored or merely covered up. They need the stitching hand of Jehovah Rapha—the Lord who heals—to close them, seal them, and restore us to wholeness.

This means that when the glory and light of Jesus penetrate those wounded places in us, He is not just easing the pain. He is stitching shut the very opening that once gave the enemy access. Healing is not only about comfort—it is about closure, restoration, and protection from future invasion.

Relationship over Systems

At the very heart of Christianity is not a formula, not a system, and not a set of steps to material gain—it is a living relationship with God. Sadly, much of what is preached today focuses on "how to get your breakthrough," "how to receive your car, your house, your next level." These things may sound appealing, but they reduce the Christian life to transactions instead of transformation.

The truth is, God never designed us to approach Him as a vending machine. He is not waiting for us to press the right buttons of prayer and fasting so we can get what we want. He is our Father. And like any father, He longs for genuine intimacy with His children. Imagine a father whose son or daughter only ever called when they needed money or a favor. That relationship would be shallow and heartbreaking. Yet, many believers treat God the same way—only showing up in prayer when there is a need.

But Christianity is so much more. God desires fellowship, communion, and intimacy. He wants to walk with us in the cool of the day, to hear the details of our lives, to counsel us, to heal us, and to shape us with His wisdom. He doesn't just want to fix our problems—He wants to sit with us in them, teaching us discernment and guiding us into peace.

The application is simple: set aside time to simply be in His presence. Not with a list of requests, but with openness. Bring Him your struggles, your questions, your fears. Let Him counsel you like a Father who knows exactly how to guide His child. This is the essence of true Christianity—relationship, not systems.

Personal Example: Spiritual Warfare Encounter

I remember being in a store one day, just going about my business, when I began talking to someone I knew. On the surface, it seemed like a normal conversation, but suddenly I felt uneasy in my spirit. It was as though warfare had broken out all around me, and I could feel something pressing against me that I was not ready to fight.

At first, I thought it must have been witchcraft coming off the other person. I had felt that before in different encounters—like a heavy, oppressive atmosphere that seemed to come from someone else. But as I prayed and asked the Lord what was happening, He spoke something that shifted my entire understanding. He said, *"It's not just what's on them—it's what's in you. That same wound, that same spirit is also in you, and it's being activated."*

That revelation hit me hard. It wasn't just about the other person carrying something demonic; it was about common ground. The spirit was able to agitate me because it recognized something familiar inside me. And that's when the Lord reminded me of Jesus' words: *"The prince of this world is coming, but he has nothing in Me"* (John 14:30). Jesus had no unhealed wounds, no hidden agreements, no unresolved sin that the enemy could grab onto.

The principle is clear: spirits can only attach where they find something in common. Deliverance cannot just be about rebuking what's on the outside; it must begin with healing what's on the inside. That moment in the store taught me that inner healing and deliverance go hand in hand. Before we can walk in authority over demonic spirits, we must allow the Lord to heal the wounds in our own souls.

The Beams of Light: Meditating on Light Scriptures

One of the most powerful applications of Malachi 4:2 is learning how to meditate on the light of Christ. The Scripture says, *"The Sun of Righteousness shall arise with healing in His wings and beams."* Those beams of light are not just poetic imagery; they are the very medicine and remedy for our body and soul. Healing comes when we learn to position ourselves in the presence of Jesus and allow His beams of light to penetrate the areas of wounding.

This is not just a mental exercise—it is an act of faith. When you close your eyes in prayer and begin to meditate on the Word of God, see with your spiritual imagination the beams of Christ's light shining into the places of your life that need healing. For example, if someone is dealing with a physical injury like my brother Steve with his knee, you can visualize those beams of light penetrating the joint, touching the cartilage, the ligaments, the tendons, the bones, and the nerves. Picture the "Sun of Righteousness" shining His healing into that very area. As you do this in faith, you are applying the Word as medicine, just as Malachi describes.

But this is not only for physical healing. It works for the soul as well. Those beams of light are also for the mind, the will, and the emotions. If you are carrying wounds of rejection, fear, or anger, picture the light of Christ breaking through those dark places and stitching them shut. Jehovah Rapha heals not only the body but the soul—He is the Great Physician who mends by stitching the open wounds of life until they are made whole.

This practice becomes what I call "relationship sessions." It is time set apart where you come before the Lord with unveiled face, staring into the face of Christ, and allowing His glory-light to transform you from the inside out. Paul said in 2 Corinthians 3:18 that we are changed "from glory to glory" as we behold Him. These beams of light are part of that transformation. They bring freedom, joy, and wholeness, because the more you sit in His presence and meditate on His light, the more healed and whole you will become.

Transformation from Glory to Glory (2 Corinthians 3:18)

Paul says in 2 Corinthians 3:18, **"But we all, with unveiled face, beholding as in a glass the glory of the Lord, are changed into the same image from glory to glory, even as by the Spirit of the Lord."** This is one of the most powerful truths in Scripture about how transformation happens in the life of a believer.

Notice the phrase "with unveiled face." That means we come before God with transparency, with nothing hidden. We bring the places of shame, the wounds we try to cover, and even the secret struggles we don't want anyone else to know about. When we bring these places into His light, the veil comes off, and we behold Him as He truly is. And as we behold Him, the Spirit of the Lord changes us—not by our effort, but by His glory.

The Amplified Bible makes it even clearer: **"And all of us, as with unveiled face, [because we] continued to behold [in the Word of God] as in a mirror the glory of the Lord, are constantly being transfigured into His very own image in ever-increasing splendor and from one degree of glory to another; for this comes from the Lord [Who is] the Spirit."**

This isn't a one-time event. It is a continual process: *constantly being transfigured, from one degree of glory to another.* God reveals greater realms of His glory to those who remain faithful, who continue to seek Him in transparency and intimacy.

I remember one particular vision the Lord gave me while in prayer. I was suddenly in what felt like an ancient place—so old, it reminded me of something out of *Raiders of the Lost Ark*. The Spirit lifted me before a great wall covered in inscriptions I had never seen before. The writing was mysterious, otherworldly, almost alive.

I thought to myself, *"I need to write this down so I can remember it,"* but in that moment I realized I wasn't dreaming—I was fully conscious, caught up in the Spirit. Then suddenly, I was taken down what seemed like a long tunnel, built of ancient bricks, filled with radiant light. I moved with incredible speed through this tunnel of light, and just as I thought I was about to enter into a new realm, I woke up. The timing frustrated me, but I knew God had given me a glimpse of something greater—a call to hunger for more of His glory.

That is what Paul is describing. As we are faithful to stay in relationship, God will entrust us with deeper encounters, greater realms of glory, and higher degrees of His presence. Each time, we are changed, marked, and transfigured a little more into His likeness. This is what it means to go from *glory to glory*.

The call is this: live unveiled before Him. Don't hide. Don't pretend. Bring everything into His light. And as you do, you will step into greater encounters with His glory, until the day you see Him face to face.

Ministry of Reconciliation (2 Corinthians 4:1-2)

Paul continues **in 2 Corinthians 4:1-2, "Therefore, since we have this ministry, as we have received mercy, we do not lose heart. But we have renounced the hidden things of shame, not walking in craftiness nor handling the word of God deceitfully, but by manifestation of the truth commending ourselves to every man's conscience in the sight of God."**

This is what Paul calls the ministry of reconciliation. At its core, our ministry is not titles, platforms, or positions—it is reconciliation. Reconciliation with God through Jesus Christ, and reconciliation with one another as His body. And this ministry only works through relationship.

But notice how it begins: Paul says we must *renounce the hidden things of shame*. That means dealing with the secret places in our soul—the things we would rather hide, the thoughts, feelings, and desires that don't line up with Christ. In the Amplified Bible it says: *"We have renounced disgraceful ways—secret thoughts, feelings, desires, and underhandedness."* That defines the realm of the soul: mind, will, and emotions. Those are the places where wounds hide, and those wounds create open doors for the enemy.

When we bring those hidden things into the light and are transparent before Christ, He can begin the work of exchange. This is the essence of reconciliation—He takes the bad out, and He puts the good in. He removes the shame, the torment, the secret bondage, and in its place He imparts His peace, His righteousness, and His Spirit.

This doesn't happen through formulas. It happens in His glory. Every time we enter His presence unveiled and honest, we are changed. Every time we sit with Him, He heals, restores, and reconciles us. And as we live this way before Him, we are then able to minister reconciliation to others—not through preaching at them, but by leading them into the same encounter with His glory that is transforming us.

Biblical Examples of Light and Glory

Throughout Scripture, light and glory are always connected. Wherever God's glory appears, His light radiates. And wherever His light shines, His glory is revealed. The two cannot be separated.
Take Moses for example. In Exodus 33, he asked God, *"Show me Your glory."* And God responded that no man could see His face and live. Instead, He placed Moses in the cleft of the rock and allowed him only to see His back as His glory passed by. Even that brief glimpse of the overwhelming light of God was almost too much for Moses to bear. And the result? When Moses came down from the mountain, his face literally glowed. The brilliance of that encounter penetrated his very being. People could not even look at him without

a veil. That's what glory-light does—it changes you from the inside out.

Even science has caught up with what Scripture has always declared. Studies conducted in Asia discovered that the human body actually emits a measurable degree of light. With special instruments, scientists placed people in darkness and recorded that each person radiated their own degree of light energy. Isn't that incredible? But the Word had already told us that Jesus said, "You are the light of the world" (Matthew 5:14). The more time we spend in God's presence, the brighter that light becomes.

The Transfiguration gives us another powerful example. When Jesus went up on the mountain with Peter, James, and John, the Bible says His very countenance changed. His clothes became whiter than any fuller on earth could bleach them, and His face shone like the sun. The original Greek suggests that light actually *emanated out of His pores*. Think about that—His inner glory was not just reflecting something external. It was radiating from within Him. His very being was light, spilling outward in brilliance.

These examples show us the principle: glory and light transform the human vessel. Moses carried it after meeting with God, and Jesus revealed it in fullness on the mountain. That same glory-light is what God now makes available to every believer who beholds Him with an unveiled face.

Childish Things & Maturity (1 Corinthians 13:9–12)

Paul reminds us that **"we know in part and we prophesy in part, but when that which is perfect has come, the partial will be done away." Then he**

makes it plain: "When I was a child, I spoke like a child, thought like a child, and reasoned like a child. But when I became a man, I put away childish things."

This is a picture of spiritual maturity. As we grow in Christ, the old immature ways of responding, thinking, and living must fall away. Childishness says, "I'll hide this from God," but maturity says, "Lord, here I am—naked, vulnerable, and in need of You." Greater transparency always leads to greater intimacy, and greater intimacy leads to deeper knowledge of Christ.
Paul also says that for now we "see through a glass darkly," but as we continue to walk with Christ, the veil is lifted and we begin to see Him face-to-face. The truth is simple: the more we make ourselves known to Him, the more He makes Himself known to us.

Childish faith looks for comfort without correction. Mature faith welcomes God's refining light. Childishness looks for blessings without obedience. Maturity seeks relationship even when it means surrender. Childishness hides wounds out of shame. Maturity brings them into His light so that glory can transform them.

This is the pathway from partial knowledge to deeper revelation. God is calling His people to grow up in Him—no longer satisfied with surface-level faith, but pressing into transparency, truth, and intimacy until His light transforms every part of the soul.

Relationship vs. Counsel of the World

In times of struggle, many people turn first to counselors, psychiatrists, or even television personalities like Dr. Phil or Oprah, hoping for answers to life's deepest problems. While some advice may sound good, it cannot heal the soul at its core. At best, the world can provide coping strategies; at worst, it feeds performance and entertainment rather than transformation.

The true answer is not found in sitting in man's face, but in sitting in Jesus' face. Only He can shine light into the hidden places of the heart and bring true healing. Christianity was never meant to be a system of formulas or a show for entertainment. It is about relationship—raw, transparent, intimate communion with the living Christ.
When we learn to bring our brokenness, confusion, and burdens before Him, He does what no psychiatrist or TV host could ever do. He heals, He delivers, He restores. No medication can stitch up the wounds of the soul the way the beams of His glory can.
At its heart, the Christian life is not about performance, appearance, or even "having it all together." It is about sitting before the King, hearing His counsel, and allowing His light to transform us from the inside out.

The Prophetic Word as Light (2 Peter 1:19)

Peter tells us that the prophetic word is like a lamp shining in a dark place. Just as a lamp brings clarity and direction in the night, so prophecy brings light into seasons of confusion, warfare, and waiting. Prophetic words are not meant to sit on a shelf, forgotten or doubted—they are living weapons and guiding lights.
Paul reminded Timothy to "war with the prophecies spoken over you." This means prophecy is not just encouragement, but a tool of spiritual warfare. When the enemy presses in, when doubt clouds the mind, prophetic words can be declared, prayed, and

meditated upon until they release the light of revelation into our soul.

Prophecies carry the same illuminating power as the written Word when received and applied. As we rehearse them before God in prayer, they become anchors that stabilize us, lamps that guide us, and weapons that cut through demonic lies. The prophetic word brings clarity, wisdom, and understanding when we treat it as light.

The Eye as the Lamp of the Body (Luke 11:33–36)

Jesus taught that the eye is the lamp of the body—the gateway through which light enters. If our eye is single, meaning focused and pure, our whole body will be full of light. But if our eye is evil, our body becomes full of darkness. This is why Scripture warns us to guard carefully what we allow through the eye gate.

There is also a warning about false light. Satan disguises himself as an angel of light, offering deceptive images, philosophies, and entertainment that appear good but actually usher in darkness. Much of what passes through our media—TV shows, movies, social media images—can carry spiritual corruption that quietly feeds our soul with fear, lust, violence, or despair.

The power of imagination proves how real this principle is. Even a dream image can trigger physical reactions in the body—your heart rate may rise, emotions may flare, and your body can even respond as if the experience actually happened. If that is possible in the negative, how much more can the Spirit of God use holy imagination for healing?

When we deliberately fill our eyes with Christ—His Word, His presence, His light—the effect is just as real. Meditating on the light of Christ is not empty visualization; it is faith in action. As we picture His light shining into wounded places of our soul, His healing presence penetrates and restores us from the inside out.

Arise and Shine (Isaiah 60:1–3)

The prophet declares, **"Arise, shine, for thy light is come, and the glory of the Lord is risen upon thee."** This is not a poetic suggestion—it is a divine command and prophetic invitation. The moment the light of Christ enters, the glory of God rises, and the two always come together. Glory and light are inseparable. Wherever His glory manifests, His light breaks forth, driving out darkness and restoring what was broken.

The glory is not confined to heaven. Heaven is a fixed place, but glory is the atmosphere of God's presence—and it can manifest anywhere. I have seen it fall in places where people least expect it: in a Walmart aisle, in a lunchroom at work, even at the bus stop. The glory of God is not bound by location. His presence shows up when people create an atmosphere of worship, faith, and hunger.

Inside His glory are all the riches of heaven—all provision, wisdom, strength, healing, and resources needed for life and godliness. When we learn how to access and live in the glory, we no longer live as beggars waiting for heaven; we live as sons and daughters carrying heaven into the earth.

Yes, the Word warns that *darkness shall cover the earth, and gross darkness the people.* That is the reality of our times—confusion, deception, brokenness, and despair. But God's answer is not another man-made system, program, or philosophy. His answer is simple and eternal: His glory and light shining through His people.

This is also a prophetic promise: *"The Gentiles shall come to your light, and kings to the brightness of your rising."* Nations, leaders, families, and even those who once opposed God will be drawn, not to us, but to the light of Christ reflected in us. When relationship with Christ is restored and His glory fills our souls, reproduction naturally happens: conversions multiply, disciples are birthed, and revival spreads. The call is clear—rise up, shine forth, and let His glory be seen upon you.

Chapter 5

Breaking the Strong Man and the Curse

Some messages are not the kind you can just read at once and walk away. This is one of those messages you have to study. You read it again, open your Bible, write notes, and let the Holy Spirit expand the truth to you. Certain revelations come only when you meditate, when you let the Word get engrafted into your heart. That's how transformation happens.

Mark 3:27 — Binding the Strong Man

Jesus said in **Mark 3:27**, **"No one can enter a strong man's house and ransack his household goods right and left and seize them and plunder them unless he first binds the strong man; then indeed he may thoroughly plunder his house" (AMP).**

This is a foundational principle of deliverance. In order to walk in freedom, we must identify and bind the strong man. Many times in deliverance services we see demons manifest and we cast out some of the lesser spirits—the "foot soldiers," if you will. But if we never deal with the strong man, the root remains, and sooner or later that house gets filled again. Jesus made it clear: the key to spoiling the enemy's house is not chasing after every little spirit, but binding the strong man himself.

Here's the truth: when the strong man is defeated, every under-ranking spirit beneath him falls as well. But when the strong man is left untouched, his kingdom remains intact. That's why so many believers experience cycles—temporary freedom followed by relapse.

The danger is that some people begin to tolerate their strong man. They think, *"I've dealt with this issue for 10, 20, 30, even 40 years. It's always going to be with me. I'll just manage it and make it to heaven."* But God doesn't want you living in partial victory. He wants you totally free. The work of the cross is complete freedom—spirit, soul, and body.

Generational & Territorial Application

The revelation of binding the strong man is not just for individuals—it applies to families, tribes, and even nations. God doesn't release truth just so one person can be free; He releases it so that whole bloodlines and regions can be delivered. Strong men don't only attach themselves to individuals; they attach themselves to generations and territories. That's why you see entire families struggling with the same cycles of addiction, poverty, perversion, or sickness. The strong man is sitting over that bloodline.

The same principle applies to nations. A spirit that rules in one region may not have the same authority in another. This is why we must discern not only personal strong men, but also territorial ones.

The Lord gave me a prophetic word that this very revelation of healing the soul and binding the strong man must be taken into Africa. He said it would bring liberation not only to individuals but to families, tribes, and nations. When revelation is embraced at that level, entire people groups can walk into freedom. Demonic powers that once ruled over regions for generations lose their grip when the strong man is bound and Christ's victory is applied.

Example from David & Goliath (1 Samuel 17:8–10, 41–47)

Goliath was not just another soldier; he was the strong man of the Philistines. He stood as their champion, declaring that if he was defeated, the entire Philistine army would submit. This perfectly illustrates the principle Jesus taught—when you bind and defeat the strong man, his entire kingdom falls. Notice how David entered the battle. Scripture records that a shield-bearer went before him. This is a prophetic picture that faith must precede the battle. Before you face your own Goliath, faith must go ahead of you like a shield. Without faith, we cannot conquer the strong man.

The enemy's strategy was clear: Goliath cursed David continually by his gods. This is how demonic powers operate—they release decrees and curses to weaken and intimidate. But David did not remain silent. He responded with a prophetic decree, declaring how the battle would end: "This day the Lord will deliver you into my hands, and I will strike you down and cut off your head." Cutting off Goliath's head symbolized the destruction of witchcraft strategies—the severing of demonic leadership and control.

David did not cower in fear or wait passively. He ran toward the battle. Too many believers are hesitant, fearing retaliation from the enemy. But the principle is clear: when we confront the strong man in faith and in the name of the Lord, victory is guaranteed. The outcome was decisive. When Goliath fell, the Philistine army fled in terror, and Israel gained the spoils. The victory of one man who faced the strong man in faith released freedom and blessing for the entire nation.

Application: Every believer must identify and defeat the strong man in their own life. Until the strong man is confronted and conquered, his influence lingers. But once he falls, the lesser spirits lose their grip, and freedom, joy, and inheritance are released.

Ephesians 6:12 — Wrestling with Rulers

Paul reminds us in Ephesians 6:12 that our battle is not with flesh and blood. People are not our true enemy. Instead, the struggle is against spiritual rulers and hierarchies that operate in unseen realms. The Amplified Bible expands this into layers of authority:

- Despotisms — tyrant kings, what I call "desperates." These are the strong men, ruling spirits that take dominion over territories, families, and even individual souls.

- Powers under them — these are the under-ranking spirits who carry out orders beneath the tyrant kings.

- World rulers of darkness — spirits that influence systems, nations, governments, and entire cultures.

- Wicked spirits in heavenly realms — the forces that occupy the unseen atmosphere around us, seeking to block the flow of God's glory and hinder our prayers.

Our first encounters in spiritual warfare are often with these tyrant kings—strong men that establish themselves in our souls through wounds, sin, or generational iniquity. They do not usually start at the surface; they work their way into the core of the mind, will, and emotions, where they attempt to build thrones of control.

Here's a vital principle: whenever a curse is released, a demon is assigned to enforce it. A curse is not just words; it is a spiritual decree backed by demonic power. But for that curse to be effective, there must be a "cause." Proverbs 26:2 teaches us that a curse without cause cannot alight. Sin gives the curse its legal ground, its reason to land and operate. As long as the soul remains wounded and doors remain open, curses find a place to rest. But when sin is confessed, forgiven, and covered under the blood of Jesus, those curses lose their legal claim and cannot stick.

Christians & Curses

A common argument you will hear is: *"Christians can't be cursed because Jesus became a curse for us."* Yes, Galatians 3:13 declares that Christ redeemed us from the curse of the law by becoming a curse on our behalf. That is absolutely true. But here is the reality: when a believer continues living in unrepented sin, that sin opens the door again for curses to operate. The covering of Christ's redemption is perfect, but our choices determine whether we walk in it.

Think about it this way: if a Christian commits fornication, lies, or steals, the consequences of those sins still manifest in their lives. The curse of broken relationships, loss of trust, or even sickness may result. Theology does not cancel the law of sowing and reaping. Sin always brings fruit with it.

Here's an illustration I often use: Christians can have whatever they want—even demons—if they choose to tolerate them. Jesus gave us authority to resist, cast out, and live free, but if a believer entertains compromise and refuses to deal with hidden sins, they are giving permission for the enemy to remain.

Freedom is available, but it requires us to shut every open door.

Numbers 22 — Balaam & Balak

When Israel entered the Promised Land, they encountered Balak, the king of Moab. His very name means *"devastator"* or *"waster"*—a king associated with curses. The background here is critical: the Moabites were descendants of Lot's incest with his daughters (Genesis 19:36–37). From the very beginning, their bloodline was marked by generational perversion and corruption. Balak's strategy was simple: if he could curse Israel, he could weaken them so they would never walk in their God-given dominion.

Balaam's Inner Wound

Balak hired Balaam, a prophet, to curse Israel. On the surface, Balaam appeared to be a man of God. He heard God's voice and knew God's will. But beneath the surface, Balaam carried wounds in his soul. He was enticed by lust for fame, wealth, and honor. Though he declared what God said, he repeatedly returned to Balak's offers, driven by greed.

This is a picture of how wounds work. Balaam knew what was right, yet because his soul was not healed, he was vulnerable to worldly enticements. His lust connected him to compromise, just as our unhealed wounds can tie us to the very temptations that pull us away from God.

The Donkey Encounter

As Balaam journeyed, consumed with greed, his donkey saw something Balaam could not see: the angel of the Lord standing in the road with a drawn sword. Three times the donkey resisted, saving Balaam's life. Finally, God opened the donkey's mouth, and it spoke to rebuke Balaam.

Here's the lesson: when lust and distraction dominate our vision, we become blind to God's warnings. Balaam, a prophet who should have had clear sight, could not see what even an animal perceived. God, in His mercy, will sometimes allow testing situations to expose our hidden wounds so that we can repent.

Balak's Desperation

When Balaam initially resisted, Balak sent higher-ranking officials carrying greater promises of honor and wealth. This reveals a demonic principle: when the enemy sees resistance, he often escalates the temptation. The offers grow bigger, the promises more enticing, the pressure more intense.

Balaam wavered. He spoke God's truth at times, but his heart was divided. He kept returning, kept negotiating, kept entertaining compromise. This persistence to return to sin kindled the anger of God, because Balaam knew His will but chose to remain driven by lust.

Principle

The account of Balaam and Balak shows us that curses operate where wounds are unhealed. Balaam's greed and inner corruption opened the door to manipulation. Balak's goal was to devastate God's people through curses, but Balaam's personal wounds nearly made him the instrument of destruction. The same applies today: when wounds in our soul go unhealed, they make us vulnerable to both temptation and demonic manipulation.

Balak's Desperation

When Balaam resisted Balak's first invitation, Balak did not give up. Instead, he escalated his efforts. He sent higher-ranking officials, men of greater honor, carrying promises of greater wealth and prestige. This is a picture of how the enemy operates. If the first temptation does not work, he will come back with something stronger, something more enticing. The pressure increases, the stakes rise, and the offer becomes harder to refuse.

Balaam found himself wavering. On one hand, he spoke the truth of God when the Spirit came upon him. But on the other hand, his heart kept drifting back to compromise. He kept entertaining the possibility of going with Balak, of receiving the reward, of mixing obedience with greed.

This divided heart stirred the anger of the Lord. Balaam knew God's will. God had made His command clear. Yet Balaam's lust for honor and wealth drove him again and again toward compromise. His wound — the unhealed desire for worldly gain — became the very entry point the enemy exploited.

Principle

When we refuse the enemy's first offer, he will often raise the stakes. But if there is an unhealed wound in our soul, we can still be drawn back to compromise. Balaam's example warns us: it is not enough to know God's will intellectually. We must have a healed soul and an undivided heart, or else lust and pride will drive us right back into the enemy's trap.

Prophecy of Balaam (Numbers 24:10–19)

Even though Balak's heart was set on cursing Israel, Balaam found that he could not speak a curse. Each time he opened his mouth, blessings flowed instead. This reveals a powerful truth: when God has chosen to bless His people, no sorcery, no witchcraft, and no curse can ultimately prevail against them.

In his final prophecy, Balaam was carried beyond the immediate situation into a vision of the coming Messiah. He declared:

> **"A Star shall come forth out of Jacob, and a Scepter shall rise out of Israel…" (Numbers 24:17).**

This was a prophetic picture of Christ — the Star of Jacob and the Scepter of Israel — the One who would bring ultimate dominion, rule in righteousness, and shatter the works of darkness.

Through this prophecy, we see Jesus revealed as the ultimate curse breaker. Every attempt of the enemy to enslave God's people through sorcery, generational sin, or demonic decrees finds its defeat in Christ. Balaam specifically declared that Moab would be destroyed, and prophetically this points to Jesus destroying not only Moab, but every "strong man of curses" that tries to stand against the Kingdom of God.

Principle

The enemy may try to escalate, manipulate, or intimidate, but God's Word always stands firm. Where the enemy intends to curse, God releases blessing. In Christ, the curse is broken, the scepter of authority is restored, and His people are empowered to walk in freedom and victory.

Principle of the Curse

Proverbs 26:2 declares: *"Like a fluttering sparrow or a darting swallow, so the causeless curse does not alight."* This verse reveals a spiritual law: for a curse to land, there must be a cause — some form of sin or open door in a person's life. Without sin to give it ground, a curse has no place to settle.

Illustration with Two Christians

Imagine two believers:

- Christian #1 walks in daily repentance and keeps their life under the covering of the blood of Jesus. When words of cursing, witchcraft, or demonic assignments are sent against them, those curses cannot stick. They may "flutter" around, but they have no landing place. Their life is hidden in Christ, and righteousness serves as a shield.

- Christian #2, however, lives in compromise — worship on Sunday but willful sin on Monday. With one foot in the church and one foot in the world, they leave cracks open in the door of their soul. This provides legal entry for curses to land, attach, and eventually build strongholds that oppress.

Application

The key to shutting the door to curses is repentance and righteousness. When we choose holiness, confess sins, and stay covered in the blood, we close every legal right the enemy tries to claim. Living in the light of Christ ensures that no curse can alight, no matter how fierce the attack.

Practical Areas of Curses

Curses are not abstract ideas; they often manifest in practical, tangible areas of life. Scripture and experience show us clear patterns of how curses take hold when open doors are left unguarded.

1. Health Curses
Many curses reveal themselves through physical sickness, disease, or repeated afflictions that seem unexplainable. While not every sickness is a curse, there are cases where afflictions continue from generation to generation — patterns of diabetes, cancer, heart disease, or mental illness — and these may point to a spiritual root. When the cause is not just natural but spiritual, doctors can only manage symptoms while the underlying bondage remains. True healing requires closing the spiritual door through repentance and deliverance.

2. Financial Curses
The Word of God is clear: dishonoring Him in the area of finances can bring a curse. Malachi 3:9 says, *"You are cursed with a curse, for you are robbing Me, the whole nation of you!"* God was speaking to Israel about

withholding tithes and offerings. Financial disobedience opens the door for lack, debt, and frustration, no matter how hard one works. Yet in His mercy, God also provides a redemption principle. In Scripture, when someone sinned against the law, God often required an offering of redemption to repair the breach. The principle remains today: when we repent, honor Him with our firstfruits, and walk in integrity, the curse of financial lack is broken and blessing is released.

3. The Main Open Door: Unforgiveness
If there is one doorway that the enemy consistently uses, it is unforgiveness. Jesus warned in Matthew 6:15, **"But if you do not forgive others their sins, your Father will not forgive your sins."** Unforgiveness is not just a heart issue; it is a spiritual doorway. It allows bitterness to take root, which opens the soul to torment, sickness, and oppression. Time and again in ministry, we have seen physical healings occur immediately after someone forgave. Arthritis, migraines, and chronic illnesses have lifted in moments when forgiveness was released. That is how powerful this doorway is.

4. Other Doors to Curses
- Bitterness — poisons the soul and keeps wounds open.

- Rejection — when internalized, it becomes a breeding ground for lies and torment.

- Envy and Jealousy — open the soul to torment and comparison.

- Strife and Division — invite chaos into homes, churches, and communities.

Chapter 6

Hurt People Hurt People

This teaching was birthed in a time of seeking God and asking Him a very honest question: *Why is the church not growing—in maturity, in strength, or in numbers?* It wasn't just about empty chairs; it was about the lack of real transformation in people's lives. As I pressed in, the Lord began to show me that much of the church is reproducing after its own kind, and that is the problem. Leaders are often wounded. Members are often wounded. And what happens? Wounded people reproduce after themselves. *Wounded people wound people.*

Instead of reproducing healthy, Spirit-filled disciples, churches end up reproducing people who carry the same hurts, fears, and cycles of defeat. This explains why many congregations can be large in number but small in spiritual maturity. True growth cannot come from religious activity alone—it comes from inner healing. When the soul is healed, the believer is able to walk in freedom, reproduce after Christ, and raise up other healthy disciples

Problem in the American Church

One of the greatest burdens I carry is the lack of fresh, radical testimonies in the American church. Where are the stories of the drug addict who came in bound and left free? Where are the broken, rejected, abused men and women who encountered Jesus and walked away transformed? Too often, instead of seeing new converts, we are seeing church transfers—people moving from one congregation to another because they were offended, dissatisfied, or simply looking for the next new thing.

This cycle has produced a body filled with carnal Christians. They know how to attend, how to clap, how to sing, and even how to speak in church language, but they are still half-committed. They live with one foot in the world and one foot in the church. The fruit shows up in gossip, strife, jealousy, competition, and immaturity.

But Jesus set a different standard for His disciples. He said that the true mark of discipleship is not in titles, positions, or even spiritual gifts—it is love for one another (John 13:35). Where there is real love, there is healing. Where there is healing, there is growth. And where there is growth, there is multiplication of true disciples, not just church members.

Genesis 1: First Words of God

The very first words we hear God speak in Scripture are, *"Let there be light."* (Genesis 1:3). This is not by accident. Light is the divine catalyst—it is what God uses to bring order out of chaos, to spark creation, and to begin transformation. Before God spoke, the Spirit of the Lord was already hovering over the waters, carrying the weight of His glory and presence. But nothing shifted until the Word was released, and the first word God chose to release was *light.*

This sets a principle that carries through the whole of Scripture: whenever God begins something new, whether in creation or in your life, He begins with light. Light exposes darkness, breaks confusion, and makes room for order. Light is the doorway to healing, restoration, and creativity. When God wants to restore what has been broken, His first step is the same as in Genesis—He speaks light.

Healing Others Begins with Healing Ourselves

One of the foundational truths of ministry is this: you cannot impart what you do not possess. If we are still wounded in certain areas of our soul, then we cannot effectively minister healing to others in that same area. Before we can lead others into freedom, we ourselves must be free. Before we can bind and cast out spirits, we must ensure that we no longer share anything in common with those very spirits.

Jesus made it clear that His kingdom cannot be divided. Light and darkness cannot coexist in harmony (Matthew 12:25). If we are still entertaining hidden agreements with darkness, then we lack the authority to bring lasting deliverance to others. Healing others must begin with allowing the Holy Spirit to search our own soul and bring the healing light of Christ into our wounds.

Paul reinforces this in 1 Thessalonians 5:13–14, where he exhorts believers to *"admonish the idle, encourage the fainthearted, help the weak, and be patient with them all."* The phrase *"weak souls"* speaks to believers who are fragile in mind, will, and emotions. Many in the body of Christ today fall into this category. They may be bound by religion, lust, perversion, deception, or fear. Tragically, captivity often disguises itself as freedom—people believe they are free while they are still bound.

This is why healing and deliverance require more than a quick prayer. Liberation comes as deception is dismantled, lies are exposed, and bondage is broken through the power of truth. Jesus said, *"You shall know the truth, and the truth shall make you free"*

(John 8:32). Truth exposes the hidden agreements with the enemy and brings the light of Christ into the darkest places of the soul.

Only when we have first walked through healing ourselves can we confidently lead others into the same freedom. Our testimony then carries weight and authority, because we have experienced Christ's healing power firsthand.

Personal Testimony: Drug Addiction

I want to share something from my own journey to show how real this battle can be. For years, I was caught in the miserable cycle of drug addiction. When I was sober, all I could think about was getting high. But once I was high, I was immediately filled with hatred for what I was doing to myself, to my family, and to God. It was a vicious cycle of misery—wanting freedom, but feeling like chains were too heavy to break.

Many people today know exactly what I'm describing. They're tired of failing their families, tired of disappointing themselves, and tired of breaking promises to God, yet they feel powerless to stop. This is the condition of a soul in bondage. Addiction convinces us we are in control while all the while it is controlling us. It deceives us into thinking the next time will be different, when in truth, the cycle just deepens.

But Jesus gives us a picture of what true freedom looks like. In **John 14:30,** He said: **"The ruler of this world is coming, and he has no claim on Me, nothing in common with Me, nothing that he can use against Me."** That is the key. Satan could find nothing in Jesus—no wound, no agreement, no hidden sin—that gave him access.

This is why inner healing and deliverance are so vital. Authority in Christ comes when our own wounds are healed and the enemy no longer has anything in common with us. If someone has been delivered from homosexuality, lust, addiction, or any form of bondage, then that person carries a unique authority in Christ to set others free in the very area where they once were bound.

My testimony of being freed from drugs now allows me to minister with boldness to those still trapped. Because the enemy no longer has a foothold in that area of my life, I can declare with confidence the same freedom to others: *"Whom the Son sets free is free indeed"* (John 8:36).

Strategy of the Enemy: Offense & Unforgiveness

One of Satan's most effective strategies is planting seeds of offense, rejection, and bitterness—and he usually does it through those closest to us. Family members, friends, and fellow believers often wound us the most deeply. These wounds become open doors for bondage if they are not healed. This is why Jesus gave such strong commands: *forgive those who wrong you, bless those who curse you, love your enemies, do good to those who spitefully use you* (Matthew 5:44). These instructions are not optional; they are spiritual safeguards. Forgiveness closes doors to offense and keeps the enemy from planting bitterness in our hearts.

John 20:23 — Authority to Remit Sins

Jesus also entrusted His followers with an incredible authority:

"If you forgive the sins of any, they are forgiven them; if you retain the sins of any, they are retained." — John 20:23

Many captives cannot repent on their own because they are bound in deception. Their will and mind have been taken captive. In these cases, believers are given the power to stand in the gap—to remit sins, apply the blood of Jesus, and release loved ones from spiritual bondage. But this same authority can also be misused. When we "retain" someone's sins by constantly rehearsing their failures, condemning them, or refusing to release them in forgiveness, we can actually hold them in bondage. The enemy exploits this, prolonging their captivity. The application is simple but powerful: *Decree forgiveness over your loved ones. Plead the blood of Jesus over their lives. Release them into freedom, even when they cannot release themselves.*

2 Timothy 2:25–26 — Held Captive by the Devil

Paul explains that many people are unable to repent because their will and mind have been taken hostage:
"...in the hope that God may grant them repentance, leading them to a knowledge of the truth, and that they may come to their senses and escape the snare of the devil, having been taken captive to do his will." — 2 Timothy 2:25-26

This is why ministry to the bound requires gentleness, patience, and intercession. It is not about arguing someone into change but shining the light of Christ into their soul until deception is broken.

Illustration: Light in Intercession

One testimony described how a believer, while praying for her brother, envisioned bringing him before the throne of God. As she prayed, she saw the light of Christ shining into his soul. Though he resisted outwardly, the light began to pierce the darkness within him. This is prophetic intercession—standing in the gap, applying the light and blood of Jesus until the captive can see truth and respond. The promise is sure: *"The gates of hell shall not prevail"* (Matthew 16:18). When we refuse offense, walk in forgiveness, and apply the authority of Christ, even the most bound loved ones can be set free.

2 Corinthians 4:4 — Blinded Minds

Paul identifies one of the greatest obstacles to salvation and transformation:

> **"The god of this world has blinded the minds of the unbelievers to keep them from seeing the light of the gospel of the glory of Christ, who is the image of God."**
> **— 2 Corinthians 4:4**

Satan deliberately blinds the mind, which is part of the soul. This blindness prevents people from perceiving truth, even when they are surrounded by it. A person can sit in church, hear the gospel, and still leave unchanged because their inner eyes remain veiled. This explains why some seem resistant to God's presence no matter how much they hear the Word or experience the atmosphere of worship. Their inability to see is not simply stubbornness—it is bondage.

Application: believers are called to apply God's Word, His presence, and His light to dismantle blindness. Persistent prayer, intercession, and the declaration of Scripture shine light into the darkened soul, breaking Satan's hold and enabling the blinded to finally see the truth of Christ.

Matthew 5:14–16 — You Are the Light

Jesus declared:

> **"You are the light of the world. A city set on a hill cannot be hidden. Nor do people light a lamp and put it under a basket, but on a stand, and it gives light to all in the house. In the same way, let your light shine before others, so that they may see your good works and give glory to your Father who is in heaven." — Matthew 5:14–16**

Believers are the carriers of divine light. This light is not meant to be hidden, but to shine and illuminate everyone around us. Notice the word "house." Spiritually, it points to places of captivity—families, relationships, and communities bound in darkness. When our light shines, it penetrates these houses and liberates the captives.

Application: through prayer, intercession, and prophetic faith, we can *soak* the souls of our family members and loved ones in the light of Christ. As we bring them into God's presence, His light penetrates their wounds, exposes lies, and brings freedom.

Contagious Light

The enemy's power is seen in how quickly disease or sin spreads in the natural world. Yet the truth is that God's light is even more contagious. When a believer spends time in Christ's presence, they become "infected" with His glory. This is what happened to Jesus on the Mount of Transfiguration—His very face radiated with divine light. Likewise, when we are saturated with Jesus, His light overflows from us, touching and transforming everyone we encounter.
Call: Get so "infected" with Jesus that His light radiates from your life. Let His brightness shine through you until others cannot help but notice and glorify God.

Acts 4:31–33 — One Heart and One Soul

The early church carried a supernatural unity. Scripture says they were *"of one heart and one soul"* and that great grace and power rested upon them. The secret was this: they shared things in common with one another, not with the enemy. Their fellowship was rooted in Christ, not in division or selfish ambition. Because of this, the Spirit moved with freedom, miracles abounded, and the gospel spread with power.
Prophetic word: the healing of the modern church will restore this same unity. When believers lay down offenses, receive inner healing, and walk in love, the result will not be small—revival will break out in cities, states, and nations.

Call to Personal Healing

For this to happen, both leaders and members must allow Jesus to heal their wounds. Divorce, family rejection, church splits, betrayals, molestation, and past traumas have left many carrying pain. Wounded leaders cannot build a healthy church. Titles and positions cannot compensate for brokenness of soul. The truth is simple: only Jesus can heal wounded souls. Not counseling, not human wisdom, not programs—but the Son of God shining His light into our hearts.

1 John 5:6–7 — Witnesses of Light

John reminds us that *"there are three that bear witness in heaven—the Father, the Word, and the Holy Spirit—and these three are one."* God Himself is united, and His witness is light. As children of God, we are called to enter that same unity by walking in deeper levels of love and light.

1 John 1:5–10 — Walking in the Light

"God is light, and in Him is no darkness at all." To walk in His light means to live in truth, transparency, and holiness. It also means fellowship with one another. John makes it clear: true fellowship in the body of Christ is evidence that we are really walking in the light. Where there is hidden sin, pride, or deception, fellowship breaks down. But confession and repentance bring cleansing by the blood of Jesus. Then love flows freely again, and the church becomes a true family.

Key principle: fellowship is not optional. It is the measuring rod of discipleship. Jesus said, **"By this shall all men know that you are My disciples, if you have love for one another."**

Application: Healing Wounds from Church & Family

Many believers leave churches not because of brand-new hurts, but because old wounds are reopened. A careless word from a pastor, a disagreement with another member, or even a leadership decision can trigger pain from years earlier. The real issue isn't always the present event—it's the unhealed history beneath it.

Often, these wounds are reinforced by inner vows we've made: *"I'll never trust another leader again." "I'll never open myself up like that again." "I won't let anyone get that close to me."* Such vows may feel protective, but they actually fortify walls that prevent the love of Christ from flowing in and through us. True healing means surrendering those vows, letting Jesus touch the root, and forgiving those who betrayed us.

John 12:35–36 — Sons of Light

Jesus exhorted His disciples:

"Walk while you have the light... believe in the light... that you may become sons of light."

To be a son of light means more than receiving light for ourselves—it means being birthed from light itself. Our identity is now rooted in the Light of Christ. Just as natural children carry the DNA of their parents, so sons and daughters of light carry the radiance, purity, and healing of Christ wherever they go.

Final Exhortation

The call is clear: become light carriers. Let the light of Christ heal your wounds first, then allow that same light to flow into your families, friends, and communities. Healing is not meant to stop with us—it must multiply. When light heals us, it does more than mend our brokenness. It equips us to duplicate that light into others, breaking cycles of pain, rejection, and betrayal. The church of Jesus Christ is called to shine with this contagious light until whole households, neighborhoods, and cities are transformed. You are a son, you are a daughter of light—carry that light, and let it reproduce.

Chapter 7

Identifying Strong Men and Their Functions

One of the central themes in this series is the healing of soul wounds—the hidden injuries of the heart and mind that the enemy exploits. These wounds are healed only by the glory and light of Christ, who restores us from the inside out. Yet we also learn that soul wounds often become open doors for strong men—spiritual rulers who enforce curses and keep people bound.

Strong Man Over Curses: King Balak

The Bible gives us a powerful example in Numbers 22. Balak, the king of Moab, hired Balaam to curse Israel. But God overruled, and instead of speaking a curse, Balaam prophesied about the coming of the Messiah. This shows that the purposes of God cannot be overturned by the enemy.

Key Principle:
A curse has no power over the life of a believer unless there is an open door of sin. Sin is the legal access point the enemy seeks. Without it, no curse can take root.
Balaam's kingdom of wicked powers exists to enforce curses when doors are opened. Scripture reminds us that "a curse without cause does not come" (Proverbs 26:2). Curses function like birds in flight—never random, but always on assignment, seeking a place to land.

Balak represents the strong man over curses. He does not work alone but collaborates with other rulers and demonic teams. Together, they form coercive alliances to establish greater influence and dominion. This is why dealing with a single manifestation is not enough; believers must confront the strong man at the root and close every door through repentance, forgiveness, and obedience to God.

New Focus: Strong Man King Agag

The next strong man revealed in Scripture is King Agag, ruler of the Amalekites in the days of Saul. In 1 Samuel 15, God gave Saul a direct and detailed command: utterly destroy Agag and the entire Amalekite nation. Nothing was to be spared—man, woman, child, or livestock. This was not merely a battle instruction; it was a spiritual assignment to eradicate a strong man and break the power of his kingdom. However, Saul disobeyed. He spared Agag's life and kept some of the Amalekite spoils under the pretense of offering them to God. His partial obedience became full rebellion.

The Impact of Disobedience

Because Saul failed to deal with the strong man, Agag's influence lingered and began to shape Saul's own life. What followed was a tragic pattern of instability:

- Cycles of defeat — Saul's victories were temporary, never complete.

- Rebellion and stubbornness — He resisted God's word and justified his actions with excuses.

- Depression and torment — He required David's music to soothe his troubled spirit.

- Emotional and spiritual instability — He swayed between love and hatred, favor and jealousy, blessing and cursing.

Agag symbolizes the strong man of rebellion, witchcraft, and stubbornness. When left alive, he creates cycles of instability and bondage in the life of a believer. Saul's downfall reminds us that partial obedience is still disobedience, and failure to deal with strong men leaves open doors for oppression and defeat.

Link to Bipolarism, Depression, Cycles of Emotions

The strong man King Agag is spiritually associated with conditions that manifest as emotional instability and mental torment. His influence can be seen in:
- Bipolar-like cycles — seasons of extreme highs and lows, sudden switches between joy and despair.

- Depression and heaviness — recurring bouts of sadness and hopelessness, often with no clear cause.

- Mental instability — confusion, wavering, and inner turmoil that robs people of peace.

While the medical world diagnoses these conditions with natural labels, many times they are rooted in spiritual strongholds that trace back to rebellion, witchcraft, stubbornness, and generational sin.

Ephesians 6:12 — Structure of Demonic Kingdoms

Paul teaches that our warfare is not against flesh and blood but against spiritual rulers:

- Despotisms — tyrant kings (like Agag or Balak), high-ranking strong men.

- Powers — master spirits that rule under these kings.

- World rulers of darkness — spreading deception across nations.

- Wicked spirits in heavenly places — spiritual forces enforcing bondage.

These strong men do not act alone. They build illegal alliances—spiritual gangs—that work together to establish dominion over individuals, families, and even nations.

Key Principle
Victory in spiritual warfare requires more than rebuking one spirit. Believers must overthrow the entire demonic kingdom structure by first binding the strong man and then dismantling the network of spirits under him.

1 Samuel 15 — Saul's Failure with Agag

God gave Saul clear and detailed instructions: to utterly destroy King Agag and all the Amalekites, leaving nothing alive. This was not merely a military order but a spiritual assignment to break the power of a strong man.

Saul's Disobedience

- Saul partially obeyed—he destroyed much of the Amalekite nation but spared Agag and kept some of the best spoil.

- His heart turned to pride and rebellion, as seen when he built a monument for himself, celebrating a victory he had not fully carried out in obedience.

- When confronted by Samuel, Saul made excuses, blaming the people for keeping the spoil and insisting he had obeyed.

Samuel's Rebuke

The prophet Samuel delivered one of the most defining truths of Scripture: **"To obey is better than sacrifice, and to hearken than the fat of rams"** (1 Samuel 15:22). God values full obedience above outward religious rituals or partial compliance.

Key Spirits Operating Under Agag

The disobedience in Saul's life revealed the influence of the spirits under Agag's dominion:

- Rebellion — refusal to fully yield to God's commands.

- Witchcraft — manipulation, control, and resistance to God's authority.

- Stubbornness — hard-heartedness, resisting change or correction.

- Pride (linked to idolatry) — exalting self, placing self above God's Word.

Spiritual Lesson

Leaving Agag alive opened the door for these spirits to continue influencing Saul, leading to cycles of instability, depression, and eventual downfall.

Modern Church Application

In today's church, the spirit of Agag is still at work. Many congregations avoid confronting sin directly because they fear making people uncomfortable. Yet, just as Saul's partial obedience opened the door to spiritual defeat, tolerating rebellion and stubbornness in the house of God hinders true worship and discipleship.

We see examples of carnal approaches where preachers try to gain attention or appear "relevant" but avoid addressing deep heart issues. One minister even delivered a sermon around the "F-word," twisting it to mean "forgiveness," while his church shouted and cheered. Such theatrics may entertain the crowd, but they do not deal with the root wounds of the soul or bring deliverance.

The principle remains the same: obedience brings freedom, while rebellion opens doors to bondage. Churches that embrace holiness, truth, and healing in Christ will reproduce healthy believers. Those that cater to comfort will reproduce wounded, carnal Christians who remain stuck in cycles of defeat.

Manifestations of Agag's Stronghold

The influence of King Agag as a spiritual strong man can still be traced in the lives of believers today. Just as Saul struggled under its weight, we see clear manifestations of this stronghold in modern times:

- Depression and Schizophrenia — Saul's later years were marked by deep depression, paranoia, and unstable thinking. These patterns reflect how Agag's stronghold breeds mental torment and instability.

- Bipolar Swings — Many believers experience drastic emotional highs and lows: one moment full of joy and victory, the next overcome with heaviness and defeat. These cycles mirror the up-and-down oppression tied to Agag's kingdom.

- Resistance to Prayer, Worship, and Fellowship — When this stronghold is active, even simple disciplines like attending church, lifting hands in worship, or spending time in prayer feel like an impossible burden. Believers under its grip feel "stuck" and robbed of spiritual hunger.

- Witchcraft, Manipulation, and Control — Agag's realm operates through rebellion, witchcraft, and stubbornness. This manifests as manipulation of people, attempts to control circumstances by fleshly means, or an ongoing resistance to God's order and authority.

Agag's stronghold is designed to wear down the soul, weaken faith, and keep believers from walking in the freedom and dominion Christ has already provided.

Mark 9:16–29 — Deaf and Dumb Spirit in Boy

In Mark 9:16–29, we see a vivid example of how spiritual strongholds manifest in physical and emotional affliction:

- Physical Manifestations — The boy convulsed, foamed at the mouth, and ground his teeth. These symptoms resembled epilepsy, yet Jesus revealed the true source: an *unclean spirit.*

- Spiritual Diagnosis — While medicine may label such conditions, Jesus looked beyond the natural to the spiritual root. The child was not merely sick; he was oppressed by a deaf and dumb spirit.

- Authority and Faith Required — The disciples were unable to deliver the boy, showing that deliverance requires more than ritual. Jesus emphasized that *authority must be coupled with faith.*

- Prayer and Fasting — Jesus declared that *"this kind"* only comes out by prayer and fasting. This discipline does not change the afflicted person but aligns the minister—sharpening faith, breaking unbelief, and tuning the ear to God's wisdom.

- Parental Insight — The father cried out, *"Lord, I believe; help my unbelief."* Deliverance began with honesty and confession. His humility opened the door for God's power to move.

- Application — Many afflictions in children are tied to generational curses rooted in witchcraft, rebellion, stubbornness, or idolatry. These strongholds gain access through family lines, but can be broken by the authority of Christ, prayer, and faith-filled intercession.

Principle: Deliverance flows through alignment with God's authority. Honest confession, combined with faith and fasting, breaks the cycle of bondage and restores freedom.

Example of Deliverance

During ministry, a woman was set free the moment the "Agag spirit" was named. As soon as it was identified, the generational witchcraft flowing from her mother was broken, and she felt tangible release—describing it as tentacles lifting from her head. This demonstrates the power of revelation and naming the strong man for what it is. Deliverance comes when hidden roots are exposed.

Joshua 10 — Five Kings Alliance

In Joshua 10, Joshua thought he was going to face a single king, but discovered that five kings had allied themselves together against Israel. This reveals how demonic kingdoms collaborate to resist God's people. Spiritual warfare is rarely isolated; strong men form networks and alliances, multiplying their strength. To win lasting victory, believers must not only confront individual spirits but target the strong man at the head. When the strong man falls, the entire demonic network collapses.

Isaiah 10 — The Assyrian King's Boast

In Isaiah 10, the king of Assyria boasted, *"Are not my officers all kings?"* This shows a counterfeit demonic hierarchy. The strong man sets himself up as a false "king of kings," ruling over other kings. But only Jesus Christ is the true King of kings and Lord of lords. The Assyrian boast mirrors how Satan imitates God's structure—building counterfeit kingdoms of power. Through prophetic discernment, we see that certain demonic kings rule over specific areas such as finances, health, sickness, and addiction. Recognizing these ruling spirits allows the church to wage strategic warfare instead of fighting blindly.

Closing Admonition

Scripture shows that sometimes God drives out enemies immediately, while at other times He allows them to remain in order to provoke His people to seek Him more deeply. These lingering battles press us into fasting, prayer, and revelation. Frustration is not meant to defeat believers—it is meant to drive us into intimacy with God until breakthrough comes.

Finally, healing soul wounds is essential to church growth and evangelism. Wounded people struggle to witness or invite others because they are still carrying pain themselves. But when wounds are healed, freedom flows, joy is restored, and believers become bold in sharing Christ.

Chapter 8

The Strong Man of Rebellion, Rejection, and Witchcraft

Foundation: The Strong Man of Agag

Text: *1 Samuel 15 (Amplified)*

Context: Saul was anointed as king not by God's timing, but because Israel insisted on having a king before God's chosen one was revealed.

Principle: When we push for something outside of God's will, He may allow us to have it—but often as a lesson that brings discipline.

Saul's Mission: God commanded Saul to utterly destroy the Amalekites—every man, woman, infant, and even the animals. Nothing was to remain.

Saul's Failure: Instead of full obedience, Saul spared King Agag and kept the best of the livestock, destroying only what he judged as worthless.

Lesson:

- Partial obedience = disobedience.

- When you refuse to destroy what God has commanded, you eventually come under its control.

The Nature of the Strong Man

- Spiritual Principle: To take dominion over a house, you must first bind the strong man (*Matthew 12:29*).

- Saul's failure to deal with Agag allowed the spirit behind Agag to gain dominion over his life.

- Strong men are ruling spirits that command and organize clusters of lesser spirits.

- This is why deliverance often requires more than just addressing surface-level issues.

- Warning from Jesus: When an unclean spirit leaves a person, it seeks rest but returns with seven stronger spirits if the "house" is left empty (*Matthew 12:43–45*).

Key Insight: If the strong man is not dealt with, cycles of bondage will continue, reinforced by even greater demonic opposition.

Manifestations of Agag's Stronghold

The strong man of Agag reveals himself through many layers of bondage. At the root is rebellion, which is simply defiance against God's instructions. Whenever God speaks clearly and we choose to do our own will, rebellion enters—and with it comes an open door to greater darkness.

Attached to rebellion is witchcraft. Witchcraft is more than spells or sorcery; it operates in everyday life through manipulation, control, hidden agendas, and deceit. It shows up in marriages, when one spouse withholds truth or uses secrecy and pressure to get their way. It appears in families, when children pit one parent against the other to gain an advantage. It is also found in churches, when gossip, slander, or controlling leadership seeks to influence people for selfish motives.

Another expression is pharmakeia, the use of drugs and alcohol that dull the mind and open the soul to bondage. Linked with it is sorcery—divination, astrology, and moon worship—all counterfeit spiritual paths tied to Agag's kingdom.

Alongside witchcraft is stubbornness, which Scripture equates with idolatry. Stubborn people refuse to submit, no matter how many times they are corrected or warned. Saul himself fell into this trap when he built a monument to his own honor, setting up an idol of self-worship instead of glorifying God.

Finally, this stronghold produces rejection. When God's word is rejected, the result is that God also rejects the disobedient. This cycle opens the door to feelings of rejection, which then breed accusation, slander, and bitterness toward others. Thus, rebellion, witchcraft, stubbornness, and rejection form a web of bondage under Agag's rule, keeping lives and even churches in captivity.

Saul's Downward Spiral

When rebellion, witchcraft, and stubbornness take root, the result is mental and emotional torment. We see this clearly in the life of King Saul. His refusal to obey God fully opened the door for a downward spiral of instability.

The manifestations were undeniable. Saul began to display schizophrenia and bipolar-like swings—professing love for David one day, then hurling a javelin at him the next. His soul was overtaken with fear, paranoia, and instability, leaving him unable to lead with clarity. Scripture records that he was tormented by evil spirits (1 Samuel 16:23), so much so that he could find no rest in his own palace.

The only relief came when David played the harp. As David worshiped, the presence of God filled the atmosphere, and the evil spirits were forced to retreat. This gives us a vital lesson: worship ushers in God's glory, and His glory drives out witchcraft and torment.

For Saul, the problem was not a lack of access to God's presence—it was his unwillingness to repent. Without repentance, his moments of relief were temporary. For us, the warning is clear: if we refuse to destroy rebellion, it will destroy us. But if we choose repentance and worship, we can walk in freedom and stability under the covering of God's glory.

Saul and the Witch of Endor (1 Samuel 28)

Saul's rebellion eventually drove him into complete spiritual confusion. At one point, he banned all mediums and witches from the land, declaring them unlawful in Israel. Yet in desperation, when he could no longer hear from God, Saul broke his own decree and sought out the Witch of Endor. This contradiction revealed the depth of his torment—making rules and then violating them. It was a picture of insanity and instability, a man so consumed by rebellion that he turned to the very occult practices he had once condemned.

At the same time, Jonathan—though his soul was knit with David in covenant—remained tied by blood loyalty to his father, Saul. Tragically, this compromise led to his downfall; Jonathan died in battle alongside Saul. His story reminds us that loyalty to family or relationships must never pull us out of divine alignment. True obedience to God sometimes requires hard choices that separate us from unhealthy ties. The lesson is clear: when rebellion and witchcraft are tolerated, they will eventually drive us into contradiction, compromise, and destruction. Only steadfast obedience to God's Word can keep us safe from deception.

The Cycle of Sin, Witchcraft, and Rejection

- Rebellion = sin of witchcraft. Wherever rebellion is present, witchcraft has a legal right to attach.

- Witchcraft attaches to wounds caused by rebellion. Hidden disobedience opens the soul to manipulation and control.

- Disobedience opens legal doors for demonic spirits. What is not destroyed begins to dominate.

- The cycle looks like this: Sin → Rebellion → Witchcraft → Rejection → Mental Torment.

This was the downward spiral in Saul's life, and it remains the same in the lives of believers today if rebellion is not dealt with at the root.

Keys to Deliverance

1. Repentance – The opposite of Saul's response.
- Repent for rebellion (root), not just witchcraft (fruit).
- True repentance closes the legal door.

2. Apply the Blood of Jesus – The blood cleanses rebellion and all sin.
- See the blood saturating your soul and breaking chains of control.

3. Forgive and Remit Sins of Others – Stand in the gap for rebellious loved ones.
- *John 20:23* – authority to remit sins.
- *2 Timothy 2:25–26* – gentleness and intercession bring captives to repentance.
- Application: Saturate family members in the blood of Jesus through prayer.

4. Apply the Light of Christ – Allow His beams to heal deep wounds.
- *Isaiah 60; Malachi 4:2* – His light brings healing and restoration.

5. Worship – Ushers in glory and drives out tormenting spirits.

- David's harp drove demons away from Saul (*1 Samuel 16:23*).
- Worship is contagious light (*Matthew 5:14–16*).

6. Fasting – A specific weapon against Agag's line.

- Esther's 3-day fast broke the power of Haman, a descendant of Agag (*Esther 4:15–16*).

- The three-day fast remains a prophetic key to overthrowing Agag's stronghold.

Modern Application

The stronghold of witchcraft and rebellion is not just an Old Testament issue—it is still alive today. It operates in marriages, families, and churches, often through manipulation, control, and secrecy. Many believers remain bound by old wounds from controlling leaders or from broken family dynamics. Instead of confronting sin and rebellion, some churches avoid these issues to keep people comfortable, but the result is that bondage remains unbroken. True liberation requires a return to obedience, repentance, worship, prayer, and fasting. These spiritual disciplines break the power of rebellion, close demonic doors, and invite the glory of God to bring lasting healing and freedom.

Chapter 9

Dealing with The Assyrian Spirits

In a prophetic dream, a terrorist spirit attempted to invade the house. This spirit was not merely symbolic of external danger but represented a strong man tied to personal struggle. Yet God intervened and placed a sword in hand—the sword of the Spirit, the Word of God—and commissioned it to be thrust through the enemy. The spirit was destroyed, revealing the authority given by God to overcome what seeks to invade and oppress.

In the next scene, four demonic, alien-like terrorists appeared—tattooed, skirted, and partially naked. Although they were not directly assigned to the dreamer, God again gave authority to strike them down. Their collapse symbolized the cutting down of a higher-level demonic alliance.

The interpretation of this dream is clear: God is granting victory over strong men. As these powers fall, promotion and increase follow, because the territorial spirits that sought to block advancement have been defeated. This is the fulfillment of Jesus' principle in **Matthew 12:29: "First bind the strong man, and then his house can be plundered."**

Personal Deliverance Weakens Territorial Powers

Deliverance is never just personal—it carries territorial impact. When an individual is set free from a strong man, the demonic powers ruling over a region are weakened. Jesus illustrated this in Luke 10 when He sent out the seventy disciples. They returned rejoicing that demons were subject to them in His name. Jesus confirmed their victory by declaring, *"I saw Satan fall like lightning from heaven."*

This shows us that casting out demons from people is not an isolated act—it causes a shift in the heavens. When strong men are broken within individuals, it shakes and dislodges the ruling powers in the spiritual realm that cover entire regions. Personal freedom contributes to territorial breakthrough.

Apostolic & Prophetic Warfare Strategy

The warfare of the church is not natural but spiritual. True apostolic and prophetic strategy is not found in political protests or natural debates but in intercession and revelation from the Father. Jesus never fought strongholds with human methods; He always sought the Father's wisdom and acted from heaven's direction.

The pattern is clear: deliverance begins with individuals, then flows outward into families, communities, and even entire territories. When believers are set free, their freedom weakens the grip of territorial powers. This produces a ripple effect of liberation that expands beyond one household into cities and nations.

Revival breaks forth when the ruling spirits over a region are confronted and overthrown—spirits of religion, tradition, pride, witchcraft, and idolatry. These powers bind communities in cycles of bondage, but when they are dismantled through prayer, fasting, and prophetic decrees, the heavens open and God's glory is revealed.

Foundational Scripture — 3 John 1:2

"Beloved, I pray that you prosper and be in good health, even as your soul prospers." This foundational truth shows that prosperity and health are not random blessings but are directly tied to the soul realm—our mind, will, emotions, and intellect. If the soul is wounded, fragmented, or misaligned, it will hinder external breakthrough in both finances and health. Healing of the soul must come first so that every other area of life can prosper in alignment with God's will.

Jesus' Promise to the Church (Matthew 16:18–19)

Jesus declared that He would build His church and that "the gates of hell shall not prevail against it." He then gave His people the keys of the kingdom—the authority to bind and loose on earth in alignment with heaven. Gates represent entry points and strongholds of the enemy in territories: homes, schools, finances, institutions, and entire communities.

The application is clear: the church must actively invade these gates through kingdom strategies. This includes raising up campus ministries to reach students, establishing school prayer programs to shift atmospheres, and building strength in business and economics to redeem financial gates. Wherever the enemy has erected gates, the church is commissioned to advance, occupy, and establish the rule of Christ.

First Strong Man: King Ben-Hadad of Syria

a. Historical Context
- *2 Kings 6:23–29* — Ben-Hadad besieged Samaria, producing a famine so severe that parents ate their own children.
- In Scripture, children symbolize seed: our future, finances, offerings, and time.
- Under oppression, people consumed what should have been dedicated to God. This represents how demonic pressure causes believers to devour their seed instead of sowing it into God's kingdom.

b. Open Door to Ben-Hadad

- *1 Kings 15:16–20* — King Asa made a league with Ben-Hadad.
- To secure peace, Asa gave him silver and gold taken directly from God's temple.
- This act of misappropriating God's resources opened the door for famine and demonic oppression over the land.

c. Nature of the Spirit

- The name *Ben-Hadad* means "son of the most high," yet he was corrupted.
- Also interpreted as a gambler or "lot-caster."

- This spirit represents the misuse of resources—gambling with what belongs to God.

- Its attacks target three main areas:

— Finances → devouring seed, keeping believers in cycles of lack.

— Praise (Judah) → suppressing worship and thanksgiving.

— Warfare → weakening the will to fight spiritual battles.

Alliances of Strong Men (Collusions)

Demonic rulers rarely operate in isolation. Just as earthly kings form alliances for protection and conquest, strong men in the spirit realm form collusions to reinforce one another.

- Joshua 10 — Five kings allied themselves against Joshua. Though he thought he was facing one enemy, he encountered a coalition. This reveals how strong men often work together, compounding oppression.

- Isaiah 10 — The Assyrian king boasted, *"My officers are kings."* This is a direct picture of demonic hierarchy: the strong man over lesser rulers, each covering a specific domain.

Key Strong Men and Their Domains:

- The Assyrian → Chief strong man, ruling over other kings.

- Babylon → King over bondage, infirmity, and sickness. Represents captivity to addictions, diseases, and oppressive systems.

- Ben-Hadad (Syria) → Strong man over finances. Attacks resources, praise, and spiritual warfare.

- Balak (Moab) → Strong man over curses. Uses witchcraft, enchantments, and generational sin to wear out God's people.

These kings build alliances, covering and protecting each other to resist breakthrough in the lives of believers and in territories.

The Assyrian Strong Man (Isaiah 10)

The Assyrian spirit is one of the most arrogant and oppressive strong men revealed in Scripture. He is portrayed as the chief ruler who oversees other demonic kings.

Targets:

- Hypocritical, godless people — those who profess Christianity but live in compromise and sin.

- Leaders and congregations that outwardly carry the name of Christ but inwardly serve self, religion, or hidden sin.

Given Power To:

1. Steal resources — siphoning wealth and provision meant for God's kingdom.

2. Remove boundaries — producing lawlessness, rebellion, and lack of moral restraint.

3. Afflict leaders and congregations alike — weakening both government (leaders) and the people (the flock).

God's Role:

- Isaiah 10 reveals that God permits the Assyrian as a rod of chastisement.

- This spirit disciplines God's people when they walk in rebellion, so that conviction and repentance might follow.

- Chastisement is not destruction, but discipline intended to draw God's people back into alignment.

Manifestations of the Assyrian Spirit:

- Religious compromise — maintaining outward form without inward power.

- Misappropriation of resources — diverting what belongs to God for personal gain or worldly agendas.

- Hypocrisy in leadership — leaders living double lives, saying one thing but practicing another.

- Weak men — lacking spiritual backbone, easily swayed.

- Corrupted women — drawn into manipulation, seduction, or idolatry.

- Powerless worship — services without presence, music without anointing, gatherings without transformation.

The Yoke of the Assyrian

Isaiah 10:27 declares: *"The yoke shall be destroyed because of the anointing."* The Assyrian represents a strong man of oppression that binds God's people with a yoke around their necks. But the Scripture reveals that this yoke cannot remain in place when the anointing of God rests upon His people.

The anointing brings growth, maturity, and spiritual fatness. As the church grows in strength and stature, the enemy's yoke simply no longer fits—it breaks off. This is the power of transformation in Christ: where once the enemy had control through immaturity, compromise, or wounds, maturity in Christ destroys the bondage.

Keys to Breaking Strong Men

1. Apply the Word and Light of Christ

— Isaiah 60: "Arise, shine, for your light has come."
— Malachi 4:2: "The Sun of Righteousness will rise with healing in His wings."

— The Word and light of Christ expose darkness and bring healing where strong men once ruled.

2. Repentance and Obedience

— "To obey is better than sacrifice." (1 Samuel 15:22)

— Strong men lose their grip when rebellion is renounced and obedience to God's Word is embraced.

3. Prayer and Fasting

— Jesus said some spirits only come out through prayer and fasting (Mark 9:29).
— Esther's 3-day fast broke the power of Haman, a descendant of Agag, showing fasting's power to overturn generational strongholds.

4. Worship

— When David played the harp, tormenting spirits left Saul (1 Samuel 16:23).
— Worship ushers in God's glory and drives away demonic oppression.

5. Healing of Soul Wounds

— 3 John 1:2 connects prosperity and health directly to the condition of the soul.
— Inner healing removes the open doors that strong men use to gain access.

6. Stewardship

- Stop "eating the seed" like those under Ben-Hadad's famine (2 Kings 6).
- Dedicate resources—time, finances, offerings, and talents—unto God. Proper stewardship closes financial doors the enemy exploits.

Modern Application & Vision

The influence of strong men is not limited to biblical history—they still operate today. In marriages, manipulation and secrecy often take root, creating distance and distrust. In families, rebellion in children mirrors the same spirit of defiance that Saul displayed. In churches, strong men manifest through control, gossip, and compromise, hindering true discipleship and spiritual growth.

The call for believers in this generation is clear: return to obedience, fasting, worship, and prayer as the foundations of overcoming. Proper stewardship of finances and time is also essential—when God's resources are honored, doors of famine and lack are closed. Above all, the healing of inner wounds is critical, for only healed souls can carry the weight of revival and walk in lasting prosperity.

The vision for the church is to rise as an apostolic and prophetic people who move beyond survival into Kingdom dominion. This means invading territories—schools, businesses, and nations—with the light of Christ. It looks like releasing new songs, prophetic worship, and deep intercession that shift atmospheres. It means sending teams into nations—Africa, Asia, Europe, and beyond—to break the power of religious traditions and establish true Kingdom authority.

This is the picture of a healed, mature, and mobilized church—one that carries glory, walks in obedience, and brings transformation to families, cities, and nations.

Chapter 10

The Blood and Light of Jesus

Resurrection Narrative (Luke 24:1–35)

Early in the morning, on the first day of the week, several women came to the tomb of Jesus. Among them were Mary Magdalene, Joanna, Mary the mother of James, and other faithful women who had followed Him. They carried spices to anoint His body, still grieving and expecting to find Him lying lifeless in the grave. Instead, they were met with the shock of their lives: the stone had been rolled away, and the body of the Lord was gone. Two angels appeared in dazzling garments and spoke words that forever changed history: **"Why do you seek the living among the dead? He is not here, but is risen. Remember how He told you in Galilee that the Son of Man must be delivered into the hands of sinful men, be crucified, and on the third day rise again."** (Luke 24:5–7, cf. Psalm 16:10).

These women ran to tell the apostles what they had seen, but their words were dismissed. The apostles considered their report nothing more than idle tales, madness, or emotional exaggeration. It is striking that those closest to Jesus—those who had walked with Him daily—struggled to believe the very promise He had made repeatedly. Yet Peter, restless and unable to ignore the news, rose and ran to the tomb. Stooping down, he saw the linen cloths lying by themselves. He marveled, perplexed, caught between doubt and wonder at what had happened.

Later that same day, two disciples were walking on the road to Emmaus, a small village about seven miles from Jerusalem. As they journeyed, their conversation was full of sorrow and confusion about all that had taken place. While they were speaking, Jesus Himself drew near and walked with them, but their eyes were restrained so that they did not recognize Him. This is a sobering picture: Jesus was right there with them in their grief, but they could not see Him. How often in our own lives do we walk through valleys and trials convinced that God has abandoned us, when in reality He is walking beside us the entire time?

Jesus gently entered their conversation, asking what they were discussing. Cleopas, one of the two, expressed his shock: *"Are You the only stranger in Jerusalem who does not know the things that have happened?"* They went on to explain the story of Jesus of Nazareth, a prophet mighty in word and deed, who was condemned and crucified by the chief priests and rulers. They admitted their dashed hopes: *"We were hoping that He was the one to redeem Israel."* To them, the cross looked like defeat, not knowing it was the very instrument of victory.

Patiently, Jesus began to open the Scriptures to them, starting with Moses and the Prophets. He explained that it was necessary for the Christ to suffer these things before entering His glory. Imagine that walk: The Author of the Scriptures Himself expounding every prophecy pointing to His own life, death, and resurrection. As He spoke, something stirred deep within them, though they did not yet recognize Him.

When they arrived at the village, Jesus acted as though He would continue traveling, but the disciples urged Him strongly to stay with them because evening was near. He entered their home, reclined at the table, and took bread. He gave thanks, broke it, and gave it to them. At that moment, their eyes were opened. Revelation came in the breaking of bread—symbolizing the body that had been broken for them. They recognized Him, and in that instant, He vanished from their sight.

Overwhelmed, the two disciples looked at one another and declared: *"Were not our hearts burning within us while He talked with us on the road and while He opened the Scriptures to us?"* The fire they felt was the Spirit of God igniting their hearts with truth, preparing them to become witnesses of His resurrection. They immediately returned to Jerusalem to share their testimony with the eleven and the others, declaring that the Lord was risen indeed.

Appearance to the Disciples (Luke 24:36–49)

That same evening, while the disciples were still gathered together in fear and confusion, Jesus suddenly stood in their midst. His first words to them were words of comfort and reassurance: "Peace be unto you." Imagine the shock of that moment. The doors had been locked, their hearts were still trembling from the reports of the resurrection, and suddenly the very One they had seen crucified was standing in front of them alive.

The disciples were startled and terrified, thinking they were seeing a spirit. But Jesus gently corrected their fear by showing them His hands and His feet, the very scars of His crucifixion. He wanted them to know He was not a ghost, not an illusion, but the resurrected Son of God in a glorified body. To further prove it, He asked for food. They gave Him a piece of broiled fish, and He ate it right in front of them. This small detail was no accident—it was a tangible demonstration that the resurrection was not symbolic but physical, real, and victorious over death itself.

Then, as He sat with them, Jesus did something extraordinary: He opened their minds to understand the Scriptures. He reminded them of everything written about Him in the Law of Moses, the Prophets, and the Psalms. He explained that it was necessary for the Messiah to suffer, to rise from the dead on the third day, and that repentance and forgiveness of sins must be preached in His name to all nations, beginning at Jerusalem. In that moment, He was not only revealing Himself to them, but commissioning them to carry the message of His death and resurrection to the world.

Yet even in this holy encounter, doubt and unbelief surfaced. Thomas, who had not been present the first time, declared that he would not believe unless he touched the scars himself. Jesus, in His mercy, appeared again and allowed Thomas to place his fingers into His wounds. But He also issued a gentle rebuke and a timeless principle: **"Because you have seen Me, you have believed; blessed are those who have not seen and yet believe."** (John 20:29). This blessing extends to us today. We have not physically touched His scars, yet we believe by faith through the witness of Scripture and the Spirit.

The Blood and the Light of Christ

From the beginning of Scripture, God makes it clear: **"the life of the flesh is in the blood" (Leviticus 17:11).** Life is carried in the blood, and because of this divine principle, the blood of Jesus is unlike any other—it carries not only life but the very light of the world. His blood was not spilled in vain; it was poured out so that the light of His glory could break into the darkness of our souls and bring healing, salvation, and victory.

When Jesus shed His blood on Calvary, He did more than wash away sin—He revealed His light to humanity. Blood and light are inseparably connected. The blood provides access, cleansing, and redemption, while the light brings revelation, transformation, and empowerment. Without the blood, we could not receive the light; and without the light, we could not walk in the fullness of what the blood has accomplished.

The apostle Paul declared in Acts 26:23 that Christ, by rising from the dead, **"would proclaim light both to the Jewish people and to the Gentiles."** The resurrection was not simply a victory over death for Jesus alone—it was the unveiling of divine light for all nations. In Him, the light of heaven broke into the earth, shining on every tribe, tongue, and people.

This is the prophetic fulfillment of **Isaiah 60:1–3: "Arise, shine, for your light has come, and the glory of the Lord is risen upon you. For behold, darkness shall cover the earth, and deep darkness the people; but the Lord will arise over you, and His glory will be seen upon you. Nations shall come to your light, and kings to the brightness of your rising."** The light of Christ brings salvation where there was bondage, truth where there were lies, healing where there were wounds, and power and victory where there was defeat.

John confirms this in his first epistle: **"God is light, and in Him is no darkness at all"** (1 John 1:5). Light is not just an attribute of God—it is His very essence. Where God's light shines, darkness cannot remain. The truth exposes lies, the life of Christ swallows up death, and the healing beams of His presence stitch up broken souls.

When we put all of this together, we see a holy pattern: truth, light, and life are one. They are not separate qualities but flowing expressions of Jesus Himself. Jesus declared, **"I am the way, the truth, and the life" (John 14:6).** And the life He offers flows through His blood. That blood shines as light into the darkest corners of our lives, cleansing shame, breaking curses, and restoring what sin has stolen.

No Sin Too Great for the Blood

One of the most powerful truths of the gospel is that no sin is beyond the reach of the blood of Jesus. His blood covers every failure, every mistake, every act of rebellion. Whether it is murder, adultery, abortion, theft, or the deepest hidden secret, the blood of Jesus is enough to cleanse, redeem, and make whole.

The Bible proves this over and over again. In the Old Testament, we see Moses—a man with blood on his hands. He murdered an Egyptian in anger, then fled into the wilderness as a fugitive. By human standards, Moses disqualified himself from leadership. But God saw beyond his failure. Through divine redemption, Moses was transformed into a prophet and deliverer, raised up to lead Israel out of Egypt. The very man marked by bloodshed became the one who carried God's law and God's presence to His people.

In the New Testament, we see Paul the Apostle. Before his encounter with Christ, he was known as Saul of Tarsus, a persecutor of Christians and a murderer by consent. He approved of Stephen's stoning (Acts 7:58–60) and made it his mission to destroy the early church. By every measure, Saul was an enemy of Christ. Yet Jesus met him on the Damascus road in blinding light and transformed him into one of the greatest apostles of all time. Paul went on to write a third of the New Testament and became a father in the faith to the Gentile church.

These biblical examples remind us that no matter how dark our past may be, the blood of Jesus is greater.

I know this personally. For years, I was trapped in the cycle of drug addiction and incarceration. My life was consumed with cocaine, weed, alcohol, and destructive choices. Even behind bars, I was still making the same mistakes, still living in rebellion. I didn't want to change, but I knew deep inside that I needed to change. One night, in the middle of my brokenness, I prayed: *"Lord, help me. I don't even want to change, but I know I need to."*

At around 3:00 a.m. in that jail cell, Jesus showed up in the form of light. His presence filled that place, and the light of Christ shined deep into the darkness of my heart. In that moment, the power of the enemy was broken, and the hell inside me had to flee. The blood of Jesus reached into a prison cell, washed me clean, and gave me a new life.

This is what the blood does—it redeems, heals, restores, and transforms. The same blood that cleansed Moses, the same blood that turned Saul into Paul, the same blood that washed me clean from addiction and rebellion, is the same blood available to you today. So, hear this truth clearly: There is no sin too great for the blood. No matter your past—whether abortion, adultery, violence, or addiction—the blood of Jesus is greater. His blood drives out the darkness, shatters chains, and makes all things new.

Call to the Church: A Righteous Remnant

In these last days, God is calling forth a righteous remnant—a people who will not bow to compromise, who will not live double lives, and who will not be content with lukewarm Christianity. Revelation 3:16 warns us: **"Because you are lukewarm, and neither cold nor hot, I will spew you out of My mouth."** God is not impressed with half-hearted devotion. He is looking for believers who burn with holy passion, who stand for truth in the face of pressure, and who live lives fully surrendered to Christ.

The key to walking as this remnant is transparency before God and man. James 5:16 says: **"Confess your faults one to another, and pray for one another, that you may be healed."** Proverbs 28:13 reminds us: **"He that covers his sins shall not prosper: but whoever confesses and forsakes them shall have mercy."** Concealed sin festers like an infection in the soul. Hidden wounds keep us bound in cycles of shame and defeat. But when we bring them into the light through confession, healing flows and freedom comes.

Jesus Himself gave us the perfect example. On the cross, He was crucified openly—stripped naked, ridiculed, mocked, beaten, and spat upon. Yet even in His open shame, He spoke words of love: "Father, forgive them, for they know not what they do." (Luke 23:34). He bore our sin and our shame in the sight of all, not hidden in darkness, but displayed in the full light of day. His vulnerability on the cross is a prophetic picture for us: if we want freedom, we cannot hide our sin. We must expose it, confess it, and let God's healing light shine upon it.

The Church today is weakened when believers try to wear masks—appearing righteous on the outside while covering sin within. But God is raising up a remnant who will walk in honesty, purity, and radical obedience. He is calling us to break free from religious facades and live transparently, not pretending, not concealing, but confessing and forsaking.

When we confess, the power of sin is broken. When we hide, the chains only grow tighter. But when we step into the light, we find mercy, healing, and deliverance. This is the call to the Church: rise up as the uncompromised, passionate remnant of God, living openly, walking in truth, and carrying His light to a world bound in darkness.

Crucifixion in the Light

The crucifixion of Jesus was not hidden in a corner, but displayed openly for all the world to see. He bore the full weight of sin, shame, perversion, violence, and lust upon His body. Every wicked act, every filthy thought, every act of rebellion was laid upon Him. And He did not carry it in secret. He carried it in the light of day, before the eyes of mocking crowds, so that our shame could be removed.

The Gospels tell us that from the sixth hour until the ninth hour, **"darkness came over all the land"** (Matthew 27:45). Even the sun refused to shine upon the Son of God as He bore the sins of the world. The darkness was symbolic of judgment—heaven itself acknowledging the weight of humanity's rebellion being poured out upon the sinless Lamb. Yet in that darkness, a cry pierced the heavens: **"My God, My God, why have You forsaken Me?"** (Matthew 27:46). In that moment, Jesus felt the full separation caused by sin, so that we would never again have to be forsaken by the Father.

At His death, something powerful occurred. He carried His own blood into the heavenly holy place once and for all (Hebrews 9:12). No longer would the blood of bulls and goats be required year after year. The eternal sacrifice was made, and His blood now speaks on our behalf—speaks of mercy, redemption, and reconciliation.

Through His shed blood, we are no longer seen as guilty sinners, but as righteous before God. His blood has transformed us into sons of light and sons of truth. The darkness of sin was defeated by the brilliance of Christ's sacrifice. Where once there was shame, now there is glory. Where once there was separation, now there is union with the Father. Where once there was condemnation, now there is righteousness through the blood of Jesus.

The Word and the Glory of God

The Apostle Paul reminds us in **2 Corinthians 3:18 that "we all, with unveiled faces, behold the glory of the Lord, and are being transformed into His image from glory to glory."** The more we gaze upon Christ, the more we are changed into His likeness. But how do we behold Him? We look into His face by meditating on His Word. The Word of God is not just ink on a page; it is the living expression of Jesus Himself.

Every portion of Scripture reveals a part of Christ's body, but the passages that speak of His light and glory are like looking into His face. As we meditate on these Scriptures, our spiritual sight is filled with the radiance of Jesus, and His glory begins to shine into us.

Paul explains further in **2 Corinthians 4:6: "For God, who said, 'Let light shine out of darkness,' made His light shine in our hearts to give us the light of the knowledge of the glory of God in the face of Christ."** In other words, when we meditate on the Word and focus on the light of Christ, beams of His glory penetrate into the deepest parts of our soul. This is more than information—it is transformation.

Application: When you meditate on the "light Scriptures," pause and visualize the beams of Christ's light shining into the dark places of your heart. Picture His light flooding the wounds, shame, and scars of your past. His glory is not just to be admired—it is to be experienced, healing and transforming us from the inside out.

Healing of Soul Wounds

Many believers have experienced forgiveness but still carry wounds deep in the soul. We can forgive someone and yet still live with the scar of what was done to us. Forgiveness removes the offense, but only Jesus can remove the wound.

These wounds often act like tombs—memorials of past pain that keep us revisiting old memories, replaying old traumas, and reliving cycles of hurt. Every time we remember, the wound seems to reopen. But Jesus came not only to forgive sins, but also to heal the brokenhearted (Luke 4:18).

The resurrection gives us a prophetic picture of this healing. Just as the angels rolled away the stone from the tomb and the body of Jesus was raised, leaving the tomb empty, so the Lord desires to roll away the stones of our soul wounds and leave behind nothing but wholeness. When Jesus heals a wound, He doesn't leave a scar as a monument to your pain—He removes it so completely that the tomb is empty.

Application: In prayer, invite the Lord into the wounded places of your heart. Say, *"Lord, roll away the stone of this tomb. Shine Your light into this wound. Remove its power to hold me captive."* As you allow His light to shine into those dark places, you will begin to experience resurrection life in your soul—healed, whole, and free.

Prophetic Prayer of Healing

In this moment of ministry, there is a prophetic call for the angels of the Lord to roll away the stones—the stones of shame, anger, rejection, abuse, and trauma that have sealed up tombs within the hearts of God's people. Just as the stone was rolled away from Christ's tomb, the same resurrection power is here to remove the barriers that keep wounds hidden and festering.

The Lord begins to put His hand on very specific wounds: molestation, rape, abandonment, absent fathers, verbal abuse, rejection, and betrayal. Each wound has become a place where darkness seeks to dwell, but the Spirit of God declares healing today.

There is an invitation to open the heart: *"Let the Light in."* Jesus says in **Revelation 3:20, "Behold, I stand at the door and knock. If anyone hears My voice and opens the door, I will come in and dine with him."** The light of Christ stands ready to flood every hidden place, if only we will open the door.

As the prophetic prayer continues, the blood of Jesus is applied—covering every sin, every scar, every memory. His blood cleanses, while beams of His light shine into the dark corners of the soul, bringing supernatural healing. This is not merely symbolic—it is the very ministry of Christ in real time.

The corporate exhortation goes forth: *"Roll away the stone. Let the light in."* What the enemy has tried to bury in silence and secrecy is being resurrected by the power of God's light.

Deliverance Ministry Flow

With the release of healing also comes deliverance. In the authority of the name of Jesus, commands are issued to every spirit tied to those wounds. Spirits of anger, rejection, shame, trauma, fear, and bitterness are ordered to leave God's people. These are not suggestions—they are decrees backed by heaven's authority.

Prophetic decrees are released with compassion: *"Be healed, son... be healed, daughter... be healed from the wounds of your father... be healed from the abuse of your past... be healed from the lies spoken over you."* Each word cuts like a sword, breaking chains of bondage.

Application is given to those receiving: *forgive your offenders, release bitterness, let go of the right to revenge.* Forgiveness is not excusing the sin, but it is breaking the power of the wound and closing the door to the enemy.

The prophetic picture unfolds: angels applying coals of fire to wounds. Just as Isaiah's lips were touched with a coal from the altar (Isaiah 6:6–7) and he was purified, so the wounds of the heart are being cleansed and cauterized by the fire of God. This is a holy purification, burning away the residue of sin and trauma so that only wholeness remains.

Testimonies arise as mothers, daughters, and women who had been abused begin to experience release. The tears that flow are no longer only tears of pain, but tears of healing as the Spirit confirms His work. The wounded are being transformed into witnesses of Christ's redeeming love.

Chapter 11

Barriers to Hearing God Clearly

Introduction: The New Move of God
In the past, many believers operated primarily by faith, stepping out with good intentions and then asking God to bless their efforts afterward. While faith is foundational, God is now calling His people into a deeper place—a season where His sons and daughters do not merely act and then seek approval, but where they clearly know His leading and direction before they move.

This new move of God is marked by intimacy and clarity. The Lord is revealing His will in multiple ways: through the gentle witness of His Spirit, through the written Word, through dreams and visions, and even through open encounters in His presence. In such moments, when God Himself speaks directly, there is no need to chase after outside confirmation from prophets, prayer partners, or others. His Word carries all the authority and sufficiency we need.

The ultimate goal is that believers would grow into a maturity where they can say with confidence, "I know my Shepherd's voice, and I follow Him" (John 10:27). This intimacy is not reserved for a select few but is the inheritance of every child of God. It is the invitation of this new move: not just to hear God's voice occasionally, but to live daily in His direction and guidance.

Barriers to Hearing God Clearly

One of the greatest challenges facing the church today is that many believers do not truly know the voice of God. They may hear sermons, read scripture, and even pray regularly, yet still lack the clarity and intimacy that comes from recognizing His direct leading. The prophet Isaiah declared, **"Your iniquities have separated you from your God; your sins have hidden His face from you"** (Isaiah 59:2). Sin creates distance, dulls spiritual perception, and blocks the flow of intimacy.

Wounded souls also play a major role. Past traumas, rejection, abandonment, or abuse leave scars that become barriers between the believer and the Lord's voice. In addition, ancestral rebellion and generational strongholds can create resistance in the spirit, making it difficult to discern God's will. Even sincere, faithful Christians often find themselves struggling to sustain a consistent, healthy relationship with Him.

The symptoms of this disconnection are sobering. Many fall back into cycles of fornication, adultery, or addictions. Others experience instability, never able to stand firm or guide others effectively. In time, some risk becoming spiritually disqualified, what Paul described as becoming *"a castaway"* (1 Corinthians 9:27). These barriers must be acknowledged and broken, for they prevent God's people from walking in the fullness of their calling and from living under the constant direction of His Spirit.

Scriptural Foundation: James 1:12–16

James writes, **"Blessed is the man that endures temptation: for when he is tried, he shall receive the crown of life, which the Lord hath promised to them that love him"** **(James 1:12).** This passage reminds us that temptation is not a rare occurrence but an inevitable reality of the Christian walk. Every believer will face it, yet each one is tempted differently—by their own unique lusts, weaknesses, and desires. The enemy studies these tendencies and fashions temptation like a personalized lure, designed to draw each person away from the will of God.

To endure temptation is more than just surviving a test—it is stepping into a greater dimension of blessing and authority. Those who resist the pull of sin are promised a *crown of life*, which represents both present blessing and eternal reward. This crown also symbolizes dominion and authority, the kingship God grants to those who overcome.

Furthermore, the crown of life is not merely a reward in the future—it is a participation in life itself, which is inseparably linked with light and truth. Jesus declared, **"I am the way, the truth, and the life"** (John 14:6). To resist temptation is to embrace His life, to walk in His light, and to embody His truth. Each victory over temptation brings believers into greater light and power, sharpening their spiritual discernment and deepening their intimacy with Christ.

The Battle of Temptation

Temptation often strikes in our most vulnerable moments—when we are alone, weary, discouraged, or surrounded by the wrong influences. The enemy waits for such times to entice us, appealing to old habits, desires, or wounds.

Personal Testimony: Even after receiving salvation, the speaker shared that he still wrestled with the strongholds of drugs, sex, and partying. The old lifestyle did not vanish instantly, and the battle for holiness was very real. Yet, instead of surrendering to shame or giving up, he learned to fight back with the Word of God. James 1:12 became his weapon: **"Blessed is the man that endures temptation: for when he is tried, he shall receive the crown of life."**

Every time temptation came, he would quote this scripture out loud, sometimes over and over, until the pull began to weaken. With persistence, the Word of God moved from being mere memory to becoming an engrafted truth in his spirit—a living reality that reshaped his responses. After months of resisting, he testified of a powerful encounter where he physically felt an angel place a crown upon his head. This was a divine confirmation that the crown of life is real, tangible, and available to those who endure.

The Crown of Life/Light Brings:

- Greater intimacy with God — a deeper awareness of His presence and voice.
- Greater dimension of power and dominion — authority to walk in victory over sin and to help others overcome.

This battle teaches us that every act of resistance builds strength, every scripture quoted sharpens our spirit, and every victory over temptation brings us closer to the crown that Jesus promised.

Temptation as Promotion

Temptation is not merely an obstacle; it is often a doorway to promotion. Scripture makes it clear that God does not tempt anyone directly, but He does allow the devil to test us (James 1:13). These tests are permitted not to destroy us, but to prove us and prepare us for greater authority in His kingdom.

When a believer overcomes temptation, it is more than just a private victory—it is a spiritual promotion. Each act of resistance builds authority, and every triumph over the enemy pushes us into a higher dimension of dominion.

Jesus' Example: Before beginning His public ministry, Jesus was led by the Spirit into the wilderness where He fasted for forty days (Matthew 4:1–11). There, He was tempted by Satan with the lust of the flesh, the pride of life, and the lust of the eyes. By standing firm on the Word of God, Jesus overcame every test. The result was profound: He not only silenced Satan but gained complete dominion over him. Immediately afterward, He stepped into miracles, healings, and the full demonstration of kingdom power.

The principle is clear: when you overthrow the strong man, every demon under his authority must also bow. Victory in temptation expands your spiritual jurisdiction. You become a vessel through which God can release greater authority in prayer, in deliverance, and in ministry.

On the other hand, repeated failure in temptation leads to stagnation. Just as Israel wandered in circles for forty years because of disobedience, many believers remain stuck at the same spiritual level. Sin robs momentum, drains passion, and ultimately leads to spiritual death if not repented of.

Thus, temptation is a test designed to either promote or disqualify. Passing it opens doors to power, authority, and intimacy with God; failing it leaves us bound in cycles until we learn to overcome.

Life or Death: Two Outcomes of Temptation

Temptation always leads to one of two outcomes: life or death. Scripture makes this soberingly clear—when we yield to temptation, it conceives sin, and sin, when full-grown, brings forth death (James 1:15). This death is not only physical but spiritual: the slow decay of intimacy with God, loss of authority, and eventual eternal separation if left unrepented.

On the other hand, when we resist temptation, we are promised the crown of life (James 1:12). This crown represents both present dominion and eternal reward. The word *zoe* refers to the abundant life Jesus gives us now—life filled with His presence, power, and peace—and the everlasting life to come.

James reminds us that *every good and perfect gift comes from the Father of Lights* (James 1:17). God's nature is unchanging, pure light. There is no variableness or shifting shadow in Him. When we walk in His light, we inherit stability, clarity, and life. But stepping into sin drags us back into the shadows, where confusion and death operate.

Living from Heaven's Resource

God desires His people to live from the resource of heaven, not the limitations of man. Too often believers rely on human wisdom, financial systems, or secondhand revelation, instead of cultivating firsthand intimacy with the Father of Lights.

I once faced a serious investment crisis that could have led to financial ruin. Instead of panicking or rushing to human counsel, he sought the Lord in prayer. In response, God gave him a detailed vision, showing the exact movement of the market. By following that heavenly strategy, not only did he avoid loss, but he prospered—and more importantly, he received supernatural peace.

This illustrates God's intention: He wants His children to live daily by His wisdom, drawing directly from His Spirit. When we rely on Him, we access strategies beyond the natural. Just as He gave Joseph dreams that positioned Egypt for survival during famine, so He longs to reveal solutions, direction, and provision for His people today.

Principle: Firsthand revelation from God is always superior to secondhand prophecy. Prophets can confirm, but our ultimate guidance must come from personal intimacy with the Father. Jesus declared, **"My sheep hear My voice, and I know them, and they follow Me***"* **(John 10:27).**

Hindrance of Sin to Hearing God

James makes it clear that temptation and sin directly affect our ability to hear God's voice. The purity of our hearts determines the clarity of our hearing. When believers persist in sin, they create legal ground for the enemy to build momentum. This momentum eventually leads to sudden death—sometimes spiritually, sometimes even physically.

On the other hand, when believers continually apply God's Word and walk in obedience, momentum builds in the Spirit. This momentum carries them into the crown of life—a place of victory, authority, and intimacy with God. Holiness protects clarity, while sin clouds discernment.

Hearing, Speaking, and Anger (James 1:19–21)

James exhorts believers to be swift to hear, slow to speak, and slow to wrath. This pattern reveals a divine order for walking in wisdom. Those who fail to listen carefully often rush into excessive talking, and those who talk too much are easily provoked to anger. Anger, in turn, produces unrighteousness and leads to impulsive, destructive decisions.

Instead of yielding to anger, the believer is called to receive the engrafted Word of God with meekness, for it has the power to save the soul. The Word must not remain external—merely something heard once or quoted occasionally—but must become engrafted, written permanently into the spirit.

Engrafting the Word of God

The engrafted Word is when scripture becomes so internalized that it shapes identity and behavior without conscious effort. For example, James 1:12— *"Blessed is the man that endures temptation"*—became so deeply planted in the speaker's heart that it was no longer just a verse, but part of his very spirit.

Engrafting the Word is like carrying the body of Christ within. Just as Christ is the Word made flesh, believers are called to embody His Word until their lives reflect

Him in thought, speech, and action. Meditating on the Word day and night (Joshua 1:8) allows scripture to penetrate deeper than memory, until it becomes reflexive truth guiding every decision.

Application: Believers should meditate on scripture until it becomes part of their identity. The closer we walk in holiness, the quicker revelation comes, and the fewer delays we experience in divine guidance.

Example: Enoch walked so closely with God that he bypassed death entirely and was taken directly into God's presence. His life illustrates the principle that consistent intimacy with God, built through the engrafted Word, results in unbroken fellowship and accelerated revelation.

Doers, Not Hearers Only (James 1:22–25)

James teaches that hearing the Word without applying it leads to self-deception. A person may listen to sermons, read scripture, or even memorize verses, yet if they do not act on what they have received, they deceive themselves into believing they are transformed when in reality, nothing has changed.

Forgetful hearers are like those who look into a mirror, see their reflection, but immediately walk away and forget what they look like. In spiritual terms, this means losing the sense of identity in Christ. The Word reveals who we are—sons and daughters of light—but without obedience, that vision fades.

Those who continue in the Word—not just occasionally, but consistently—become doers of what they hear. The result is blessing in all they do, because obedience aligns them with God's will and opens the flow of divine favor.

Walking in the Light (John 12:35–36)

Jesus warned His disciples to *walk while they had the light and keep living by it.* Light is not just revelation; it is a way of life. To walk in the light is to live in continual alignment with God's truth and presence.

- Light drives out darkness. Where light shines, fear and confusion cannot remain.

- Constant light equals protection. Just as a child feels safe when the hallway light is left on, believers are shielded from fear when they remain in God's light.

- Light must be believed and lived. It is not enough to own a Bible or hear truth; one must actively trust, rely on, and live by the light.

A practical way to do this is to use imagination and faith to sit before God's throne in prayer, inviting His light to penetrate hidden areas of the soul. When believers welcome the light, God exposes wounds, sin, and fear—not to condemn, but to heal and transform.

Testimonies:

- A young woman applied this teaching and testified that she woke the next morning with unusual clarity and inner change.

- Another believer battling a skin disease meditated on the light of God shining into his body. He later testified that the afflicted areas began to heal, confirming that God's light has power to restore even physical infirmities.

Forgiveness and Deliverance through the Light

One of the greatest barriers to walking in God's light is unforgiveness. In a powerful testimony from Africa, a woman came forward for prayer but could not experience breakthrough. As the minister prayed, he discerned that she needed to forgive someone who had deeply wounded her. Through tears, she admitted her brother had raped her. The call was given: *forgive him.* At that moment of surrender, when she released forgiveness, the light of Christ entered her soul, deliverance took place, and she was healed.

Principle: unforgiveness blocks the light; forgiveness opens the door. When we hold onto bitterness, anger, or pain, we keep darkness in place. But when we forgive, we invite the light of Christ to heal wounds, roll away stones, and set us free.

Interceding for Others

Jesus gave His disciples authority in John 20:23: *"Whosoever sins you remit, they are remitted unto them."* This means believers can intercede for others, bringing them before the throne of God, asking Him to release mercy, and opening doors for transformation.

Application: bring family, friends, children, and even those far from God into His presence through prayer and intercession. Stand in the gap, pleading the blood of Jesus over their lives.

Testimony: the minister's wife practiced this with her brother, who had long resisted the gospel. She brought him before God in prayer, remitting his sins and interceding for his salvation. Not long after, her brother began attending church, encountered Jesus, and gave his life to Him. Even more, his son came with him and was also saved. The Word worked—transforming not just one man, but an entire family line.

Living Daily in the Light

From the very beginning, God's desire has been intimacy with His people. In Genesis, He walked with man in the cool of the day. That longing for fellowship has never changed.

Yet the enemy fills believers with lies: *"God doesn't care about you. God blesses others but not you. Something is wrong with you."* These are deceptions meant to keep people from the truth.

The truth is this: God loved humanity so deeply that He gave His only Son, so that every believer could walk in intimacy with Him. The cross removed every barrier, and the light of Christ restores what sin and shame tried to destroy.

Examples of God's strategy through light and revelation:

- The investment vision: when facing financial uncertainty, the minister sought God. In prayer, God gave a detailed vision of market movements. Following that vision brought profit and peace.

- Joseph in Egypt: by interpreting Pharaoh's dream, Joseph received heavenly wisdom. That insight brought favor, preserved a nation, and led to prosperity.

Application today: this is how the wealth transfer to the righteous will take place. God will give His people heavenly strategies—blueprints from His throne—for business, ministry, family, and life. As believers walk in the light, they will receive divine wisdom to prosper and to shine as witnesses in a dark world.

Chapter 12

Pillars of Inner Healing

Introduction: The Mandate for Healing

God has made it clear: *"You've got to get the people healed because you're trying to build with wounded people and it will not work."* This word sets the foundation for understanding why inner healing is not optional but essential. Wounded hearts, broken emotions, and unresolved past issues cannot carry the weight of Kingdom advancement. If the church tries to build while the people remain unhealed, the work will collapse under the strain.

For the Kingdom mandate to move forward—whether in a city, a community, or the nations—God's people must be made whole. Healing is not just personal; it is corporate and generational. A healthy body of believers can rise into its mandate with strength, stability, and endurance.

The very first and most critical pillar in this process of healing is establishing a right relationship with God. Everything else flows from this foundation. Without it, true inner healing cannot be sustained, and the Kingdom cannot advance as God intends.

Relationship with God vs. Religion

Many Christians today operate in religion but lack a true relationship with God. Religion offers rituals, traditions, and systems, but it cannot substitute for intimacy with the living God. A genuine relationship with Him is what brings favor, opens doors, and makes us effective—not only in the church but also in government, economics, community, and every sphere of influence.

God reveals Himself as Jehovah Rapha—the Lord who heals. Healing does not come through man-made structures but through knowing Him personally. Until we encounter Him as healer, deliverer, and restorer, we cannot walk in complete inner wholeness.

Religion, on the other hand, is built on systems and traditions. Denominations, man-made rules, and rituals may have served a purpose in a past season, but they cannot replace a living relationship with God. What once carried the presence of God becomes lifeless when turned into a system.

At its root, religion seeks to earn God's favor through works and performance. Relationship, however, receives righteousness as a free gift by faith in Jesus Christ. True freedom and inner healing flow not from striving but from embracing the love, grace, and acceptance of the Father.

The Danger of Religious Systems

Religious systems, often perpetuated through denominations such as Baptist, Pentecostal, Methodist, and others, can subtly replace the Spirit with tradition. When people depend on systems instead of intimacy with God, compromise becomes normalized. Churches can form "good old boy clubs" that excuse gossip, backbiting, immorality, drinking, or other sins because leaders themselves model and tolerate them. These systems numb people to the "little foxes" that destroy the vine, teaching them to overlook the very things that slowly corrode holiness and intimacy with God.

Jesus raised the standard far beyond what systems require. The Law said, *"Do not kill,"* but the Spirit revealed that anger and harsh words are murder in the heart. The Law commanded, *"Do not commit adultery,"* but the Spirit exposed that a lustful look is adultery in the heart. Systems focus on external behavior, but the Spirit goes deeper to heal the root motives. Churches led by systems fall into dead religion, while churches led by the Spirit walk in life, healing, and true transformation.

The Call to Personal Relationship

Leaders cannot stand in place of people's intimacy with God. Just as Israel told Moses to speak to God for them, many Christians rely on pastors or prophets instead of seeking Him for themselves. But every believer is called to pursue personal fellowship with God.

Each believer must:

- Seek God directly in prayer and the Word.

- Know Him as healer, deliverer, and revealer of mysteries.

- Minister to others out of overflow from that relationship, not dependency on man.

Without relationship, even religious activity is empty. Jesus warned that on the last day, many will say, *"Lord, Lord, did we not do mighty works in Your name?"* but He will answer, *"I never knew you."* The true call is not to perform systems but to walk daily in intimate relationship with Him.

The Power of the Word in Relationship

Romans 3:22–25 reminds us that we are justified freely by God's grace through the redemption that is in Christ Jesus. This justification is not something we earn through works or religious effort—it is a gift received by faith. True transformation flows from the living Word, not external systems.

When the Word is meditated on deeply, it brings light and begins to transform the heart. The Word must be more than something we hear or recite; it must be engrafted into our spirit, becoming part of who we are. Ownership of the Word happens when God Himself writes it on the tablets of our hearts, making it function like a living organ within us. This engrafted Word is literally part of the body of Christ dwelling in us. When Spirit and Word come together, true change occurs—not outward conformity to religious systems, but inward transformation by divine power.

Fear, Religion, and Wrong Identity

Religion always produces fear, torment, and a sense of unworthiness before God. Many Christians dislike themselves, and in doing so they reject the very image of God in which they were created. Instead of embracing God's love, they live under shame and condemnation.

The truth is that sin within is not your true identity—it is an invading demonic force. Evil spirits entwine themselves with personality, deceiving people into believing, *"This is who I am."* But Scripture makes it clear, as Paul said in Romans 7: *"It is no longer I, but sin that dwells in me."* The addiction, anger, lust, or fear is not the real you—it is a counterfeit attachment.

Deliverance and right relationship with God expose these lies. As believers walk in the light, darkness must flee. Every demon, every false identity, every lie loses its power when intimacy with God and the light of His Word are embraced. True healing begins when we recognize that our identity is in Christ alone, not in the sins or struggles that try to define us.

Casting Out vs. Maintaining Deliverance

Deliverance is powerful and necessary, but it is not the final step toward lasting freedom. Demons can be cast out, but without a living relationship with God, the same spirits often return. This is why many believers fall back into the same sins repeatedly—they rely on temporary deliverance instead of cultivating intimacy with Christ.

The truth is this: you are not your sin. You are not a crackhead, adulterer, fornicator, or liar. Those labels are lies from the enemy. According to Genesis 1:26, you were created in the very image of God, and everything He made was good. Sin is an intruder, not your identity. But only a sustained relationship with God can preserve your freedom and keep darkness from regaining a foothold. Relationship with Him is the key to maintaining deliverance.

Unforgiveness vs. Love

Unforgiveness is, at its core, selfishness. It clings to offense, insisting on personal justice, while ignoring the mercy God has shown us. Yet God forgives even the worst sins, and as His children, we are called to do the same.

The reason many believers struggle to love others is simple: you cannot give what you are not receiving. If someone is not receiving love from God, they cannot release love to others. Instead, wounded believers project what has been sown into them—anger, lust, gossip, bitterness. But when they receive God's love deeply into their hearts, they begin to release love instead of pain.

Love transforms environments. Where anger once spread, peace now flows. Where gossip once burned, encouragement rises. This is why Jesus, who was full of love, transformed every room He entered. His people are called to reflect that same fullness of love, carrying His heart into a broken world.

The Role of the Church in Relationship

The Church is God's chosen vehicle to advance His Kingdom on earth. It is not a man-made institution to be discarded at will—it is the very bride of Christ. Because of this, we cannot claim to have a right relationship with God while simultaneously rejecting His Church. To dishonor the bride is to dishonor the Bridegroom.

In today's culture, many have embraced the idea of being "internet Christians," replacing fellowship with podcasts, livestreams, and recorded messages. While these tools can supplement, they can never substitute the gathering of the saints. It is in God's house that worship, order, accountability, and corporate alignment in the Spirit take place. Jesus Himself declared, **"On this rock I will build my church, and the gates of hell shall not prevail against it" (Matthew 16:18).** The Church remains the place of equipping, strengthening, and advancing God's Kingdom purposes.

Healing Emotional Wounds through Relationship

True healing of the heart cannot be achieved through religious systems or external works. Only a non-religious, intimate relationship with God can dissolve the defense mechanisms we build from past pain. Religion may produce activity, but it cannot heal the soul. Only love received in relationship with Christ brings lasting transformation.

1 Corinthians 1:9 tells us that we are called into fellowship with Jesus Christ. This fellowship is not optional—it is the very lifeline of healing. Fear of intimacy with God often keeps believers bound in shame and brokenness, but the truth is that His presence brings freedom, deliverance, blessing, and joy. In relationship, God rolls away the stones of emotional wounds and replaces them with His peace. It is in His love that the deepest scars are healed, and the believer is restored to wholeness.

Chapter 13

Pillars of Inner Healing Cont.

God has spoken a clear and sobering word: *"You've got to get the people healed because you're trying to build with wounded people and it will not work."* This truth cuts to the heart of why so many efforts in churches, communities, and even nations collapse before they can bear lasting fruit. When people remain bound, broken, and wounded in spirit and soul, they cannot carry the weight of Kingdom responsibility.

Healing is not optional—it is essential. For the city, the community, and the nations to advance in the Kingdom mandate, the people of God must first be restored and made whole. A wounded people cannot effectively embrace their calling. The Church cannot advance into its prophetic destiny while carrying the baggage of unresolved pain, unforgiveness, and fractured identity.

The very first and most vital pillar in this process is having a right relationship with God. Everything else flows from this foundation. Without a living, vibrant connection to the Father, believers remain spiritually unhealthy and unequipped to fulfill their God-given mandate. Programs, systems, and religious activity will always fall short if the people themselves are unhealed. Only when the relationship with God is restored, strengthened, and made central can His people step into the fullness of His purpose for their lives and for the territories He has called them to impact.

Pillar One: Right Relationship with God

The first and most critical pillar of inner healing is having a right relationship with God. Without this foundation, everything else in life—whether personal growth, ministry, or even national progress—remains unstable. The reality is that most Christians, churches, and even nations are unhealthy because they lack this right relationship. Religion, culture, and human effort cannot substitute for intimacy with the Father. Healing and true effectiveness flow only from Him.

The prophet Malachi declared that in the last days, God would turn **"the hearts of the fathers to the children and the hearts of the children to their fathers"** (Malachi 4:6). This prophecy reveals God's priority for relational restoration. A healthy relationship with God will always reflect in the restoration of relationships within families and communities. When fathers are reconnected to their children, and children honor and receive from their fathers, the curse is broken, and the blessing of God flows.

Spiritual fathers and mentors are vital in this process. Just as natural parents are responsible for nurturing and guiding their children, God raises up spiritual leaders to develop, instruct, and impart wisdom to the next generation. This principle ensures the continuation of healthy relationships and strengthens the Body of Christ. Without fathers and mentors, believers remain spiritually orphaned and vulnerable.

One powerful example of this principle is the role of young people in advancing the Kingdom. While experience and maturity are valuable, the zeal and energy of young men and women are indispensable. They bring strength, excitement, and a willingness to labor that can fuel revival and Kingdom advancement. Where older generations may be limited by responsibilities or weariness, the younger carry an untamed energy that God uses for His glory.

Finally, we must remember that strategy comes in God's presence. Intimacy with Him not only heals wounds but also provides direction. It is in His presence that confusion dissolves, peace is restored, and clear instruction is given for the next step. Many frustrations in life are the result of trying to plan and labor without hearing from God. But when the believer prioritizes relationship with Him, He releases wisdom, guidance, and supernatural peace that surpasses understanding.

The pillar of right relationship with God is non-negotiable. Without it, inner healing is impossible, and Kingdom advancement will always fall short.

Pillar Two: Right Relationship with Self

The second pillar of healing is developing a right relationship with yourself. Many believers struggle in this area, even after salvation. They may believe God loves them, yet deep inside, they do not like themselves. They dislike their appearance, regret their past, compare themselves to others, or feel inadequate because of money, knowledge, or status. Modern media and culture intensify this struggle, feeding false standards of beauty, success, and identity. The result is self-hatred, insecurity, and a constant sense of unworthiness.

But the truth is this: identity comes only through God. Until a believer discovers who God is, they cannot discover who they are. In Matthew 16:13–18,

Jesus asked His disciples, **"Who do you say that I am?"** When Peter declared, **"You are the Christ, the Son of the living God,"** Jesus immediately gave him a new identity: *"You are Peter, and upon this rock I will build my church."* Peter's revelation of Christ unlocked his true self. In the same way, when we know God as Father, Redeemer, and Lord, He reveals our true name, purpose, and destiny.

This truth has been confirmed through powerful testimonies. One believer shared how, while seeking God deeply in prayer, he was given an open vision. In that encounter, God not only revealed His glory but also disclosed the man's apostolic identity and global assignment to nations. This illustrates the principle: when we pursue God's presence, He strips away false labels and replaces them with His divine commission.

From the beginning, our identity was established in creation. **Genesis 1:26 declares, "Let us make man in our image, after our likeness."** We are spirit beings housed in bodies, carrying souls made to reflect God's glory. Yet over time, sin, rejection, and brokenness layer us with false coverings—shame, pride, fear, lust, or insecurity. God's process of sanctification is a stripping process: removing every false covering until the true self, made in His image, is revealed.

When this happens, a believer receives not only identity but also authority. Scripture shows that true identity gives us a spiritual name that carries weight in the unseen realm. Acts 19 describes how demons recognized Paul's authority but mocked the sons of Sceva because they had no true identity in Christ. Demons know when someone is walking in their God-given name, and they must submit to that authority.

Finally, relationship with God restores us to the dominion first given in Eden. Genesis 1:28 declares God's mandate: **"Be fruitful and multiply, replenish the earth, and have dominion."** When we embrace who we are in Christ, we regain spiritual authority over creation, circumstances, and the enemy's schemes. No longer bound by comparison or insecurity, we step into the confidence of being sons and daughters of God, bearing His image and carrying His dominion.

Healing begins when you see yourself as God sees you—redeemed, chosen, and empowered. Only then can you truly walk in freedom and authority.

The Word, Identity, and Doing

James 1:23–25 makes a sharp distinction between merely hearing the Word and actually doing it: **"For if any be a hearer of the word, and not a doer, he is like a man beholding his natural face in a glass: for he beholdeth himself, and goeth his way, and straightway forgetteth what manner of man he was. But whoso looketh into the perfect law of liberty, and continueth therein, he being not a forgetful hearer, but a doer of the work, this man shall be blessed in his deed."**

This passage connects identity directly with action. The mirror is the Word of God—it reflects who we truly are in Christ. But if we only glance at it and walk away without living it, we forget our identity. Doing the Word confirms and strengthens identity. Just as a judge's identity is proven by judging, a builder's by building, and a believer's by believing, so too the Christian's identity is confirmed by living out the Word.

The Word must not remain external; it must be engrafted into the heart—owned, absorbed, and internalized—so that it becomes part of who we are. When the Word is engrafted, it releases power, transformation, and blessing. Without this, faith becomes vague and powerless. For example, healing cannot be received by saying, *"I believe God can heal."* It must be grounded in the specific Word: *"By His stripes I am healed" (Isaiah 53:5).* Standing on a revealed Word unlocks the blessing promised.

Right Relationship with Self (Continued)

A right relationship with self is inseparable from identity in the Word. When believers know who they are in Christ, they walk in confidence, free from destructive comparisons. Confidence in God-given identity is the foundation of a healthy self-relationship.

Self-hate, on the other hand, is one of the most destructive forces in the believer's life. It is rooted in demonic deception, convincing people they are worthless, ugly, or hopeless. Many mental and physical infirmities—including depression, anxiety, eating disorders, and even suicidal thoughts—stem from this deception. The enemy uses self-hate to distort God's image in us, binding believers in cycles of defeat and despair.

But when you begin to see yourself as God sees you, everything changes. Instead of rehearsing lies—*"I'm not good enough, I don't measure up, I'll never change"*—you embrace truth: *"I am fearfully and wonderfully made. I am a new creation in Christ. I am loved, chosen, and accepted."* (Psalm 139:14; 2 Corinthians 5:17; Ephesians 1:4–6).

Healthy relationship with self flows directly from a healthy relationship with God. When you receive His love, forgiveness, and truth, you learn to extend those same realities to yourself. You begin to forgive yourself, bless yourself, and stand strong in your God-given identity.

Evil spirits exploit self-hate because it provides a foothold. When believers dislike themselves, they open the door to cycles of sin, addiction, sickness, and despair. But when self-relationship is healed by God's love, those cycles break. Light enters, darkness flees, and believers walk in freedom and authority.

Pillar Three: Right Relationship with Others

Fellowship is one of the great pillars of ministry. God never designed the Christian walk to be lived in isolation. Relationships with others are not optional—they are vital. Yet for many believers, relationships are the very area of deepest pain. Because so many grew up without healthy models of family love, they carry broken patterns of communication, mistrust, and dysfunction into their adult lives and even into the church. Instead of life-giving fellowship, relationships often become a source of conflict, disappointment, and wounds.

At the root of most relational dysfunction is unforgiveness. Jesus was direct about this in **Matthew 6:14–15: "For if ye forgive men their trespasses, your heavenly Father will also forgive you: But if ye forgive not men their trespasses, neither will your Father forgive your trespasses."** Our fellowship with God is directly tied to how we treat others. If we withhold forgiveness, we block the flow of God's grace in our own lives.

Unforgiveness is more than an emotional wound—it is a spiritual chain. It means we do not trust God to judge righteously or to vindicate us. By holding onto bitterness, we assume the role of judge, jury, and executioner. But Scripture is clear: **"Vengeance is mine; I will repay, saith the Lord"** (Romans 12:19). Refusing to forgive is not only disobedience; it is unbelief in God's justice.

This reality became personal in my own journey. I had to confront my father's deep unforgiveness. For years, bitterness poisoned his relationships and hardened his heart. But through prayer, persistence, and the grace of God, he eventually repented and reconciled. It was not an easy process, but it demonstrated the liberating power of forgiveness—not only for the one who forgives but also for the one who receives it.

The consequences of unforgiveness are severe. Scripture warns that refusing to forgive others can keep a person in spiritual bondage and, ultimately, out of heaven. To live in unforgiveness is to align with tormentors rather than with God's love (see Matthew 18:34–35). That is why forgiveness is not optional; it is essential.

Forgiving others does not mean excusing their actions or denying the pain they caused. It means releasing them into God's hands, trusting Him to be the righteous Judge, and choosing freedom for ourselves. Forgiveness restores fellowship, heals relationships, and keeps us aligned with the Father's heart.

Handling Offenses

Offenses are not optional—they are inevitable. In families, workplaces, friendships, and even the church, opportunities for offense will always arise. Jesus warned plainly: "It is impossible but *that offences will come*" (Luke 17:1). The issue is not whether offense will happen, but how we choose to respond when it does.

The success or failure of our relationships often hinges on our response to offense. Offense is one of the enemy's most effective tools to divide, isolate, and destroy. His strategy is simple: create a two-for-one destruction. If he can ensnare both the offender and the offended with bitterness, unforgiveness, or pride, he succeeds in breaking fellowship and stunting the flow of God's Spirit.

The Christlike response to offense is humility. Apologizing when we are wrong—and even when we believe we are right—diffuses conflict and opens the door to restoration. Humility invites the Spirit of God to intervene where pride would keep the door closed. Sometimes maturity means choosing reconciliation over vindication, laying down our "right" to be right in order to preserve peace and unity.

Maturity is required to restore relationships regardless of who caused the offense. Paul exhorted believers: *"As much as lieth in you, live peaceably with all men"* (Romans 12:18). This requires intentional effort, forgiveness, and the willingness to reach out even when it feels undeserved.

Christ's Example in Relationships

The ultimate model of handling offenses is Jesus Himself. He bore sins He never committed, carrying the blame and punishment for the guilty in order to reconcile humanity to God. At the cross, He demonstrated the highest form of humility: absorbing the ultimate offense in order to restore broken relationship.

Believers are called to mirror this nature. We are living sacrifices (Romans 12:1), willing to lay down pride, grudges, and demands for justice to preserve unity in the body of Christ. Relationships are too valuable to be discarded over misunderstandings or offenses. God calls us to build bridges, not burn them.

True spirituality is not measured by how many Scriptures we can quote or how loudly we can pray, but by our willingness to restore relationships—even when we are "in the right." To walk like Christ means embracing His heart for reconciliation above self-preservation.

Offense will come, but offense does not have to stay. Christlike humility and love turn stumbling blocks into stepping stones, preserving unity and releasing the healing flow of God.

www.ingramcontent.com/pod-product-compliance
Lightning Source LLC
Chambersburg PA
CBHW060538100426
42743CB00009B/1564